HOLOCAUST REFUGEES IN VIRGINIA

THE STORY OF THE SS *QUANZA*

JASON NORMAN

Published by The History Press
An imprint of Arcadia Publishing
Charleston, SC
www.historypress.com

Front cover: After passengers on the SS *Quanza* were turned away from both New York and Mexico, Norfolk represented their last hope of escape from Nazi Germany in the summer of 1940. *Courtesy of Norfolk Public Library.*

First published 2025

Manufactured in the United States

ISBN 9781467159593
Hardcover ISBN 9781540299895

Library of Congress Control Number: 2025943121

CONTENTS

FOREWORD

Around 1990, my uncle David E. Morewitz, a tax attorney and accountant in New York City, started to send me documents from the U.S. National Archives and the U.S. Immigration and Naturalization Service about the history of the steamship *Quanza*. I believe he wanted me to do something with the documents, but he never told me specifically what he wanted.

In 1990, little was known about the history of the Portuguese ship SS *Quanza*, which, in September 1940, was anchored in the harbor of Hampton Roads, Virginia, carrying mostly Jewish refugees who were desperately seeking sanctuary from Nazi Europe. The Jewish refugees were going to be sent back to Nazi Europe and face death in the Nazi concentration camps.

I decided to use these government documents to begin researching the 1940 history of the SS *Quanza* controversy. I discovered that my grandparents, admiralty attorneys Jacob L. (J.L.) Morewitz and Sallie Rome (S.R.) Morewitz, had the *Quanza* arrested in Norfolk, Virginia, using an admiralty libel suit in U.S. District Court in Norfolk, Virginia (opinion from the bench, *Moritz Rand et al. v. Steamship "Quanza,"* in Admiralty No. 6594, U.S. District Court for the Eastern District of Virginia, Norfolk Division, January 22, 1943). I discovered that my grandparents' admiralty libel lawsuit helped to alter the course of history because Assistant Secretary of State Breckinridge Long retaliated against the refugee advocates who rescued the *Quanza* survivors by significantly reducing immigration of European refugees fleeing the war and Nazi persecution at a time when Hitler was pushing out Jews.

My research led to several projects that brought much more attention to the history of the ship controversy and its impact on American history and the Nazi Holocaust. Around 1990, I accidentally met playwright Susan Lieberman in our Chicago apartment building's laundry room, and we decided to coauthor the play *Steamship Quanza*, which was first produced by Chicago Dramatists in 1991. It was the first play about Holocaust ship refugees who were rescued in America.

As my research expanded, I became curator of the first SS *Quanza* museum exhibit, which includes two scale models of the ship built by model shipwright Martin Meyer of Chicago. Our exhibit has traveled to different museums, universities and religious institutions. My uncle David and I helped to establish a special SS *Quanza* collection at the University of Illinois, Urbana-Champaign (UIUC). The UIUC College of Law awarded us the George Washington Cup for our work on the SS *Quanza*'s history. I also provided SS *Quanza* research for a U.S. Holocaust Memorial Museum special exhibit on the National Mall, "Americans and the Holocaust."

Filmmaker Laura Seltzer-Duny, president of Seltzer Film & Video, and I collaborated to produce an Emmy-nominated documentary about the SS *Quanza* controversy, *Nobody Wants Us*. In addition, Laura and I have collaborated to develop an SS *Quanza* curriculum for schools, universities and other organizations.

Poet and novelist Victoria Redel portrayed me as a SS *Quanza* curator in her novel *The Border of Truth*. A graduate student at Old Dominion University, Stephanie Hawthorne, used our SS *Quanza* research to design a SS *Quanza* videogame for her master's thesis.

Jason Norman's book is now part of an excellent tradition of research about the SS *Quanza* controversy. Norman offers fresh, vivid behind-the-scenes accounts of the life-and-death dramas that the SS *Quanza* survivors faced while onboard the ship and, later, imprisoned on the vessel when it finally anchored in Hampton Roads. Jason Norman also delves into the lives of my grandparents as they used their admiralty law skills to delay the ship from sailing back to Nazi Europe. His book tells a rich story of heroes and survivors.

—Stephen J. Morewitz, PhD

INTRODUCTION

It's said that a journey of a thousand miles begins with a single step. It ends the same way.

But what if, after so many miles, that one last step just couldn't be taken? Imagine looking at that pier and the land just beyond it. You, your loved ones, friends you'd made on the way—just sitting there, staring at it. You'd traveled over a month to get here, thousands of miles upon miles of navigating across waves, and you'd finally made it. The land in front of you, your personal finish line? You could see it. If you could take a few steps, you could touch it. It felt like you could whisper and someone standing there would hear you perfectly well. Your long journey was a few small steps from its end.

And now something was holding you back in every sense of the word. You'd made it that far, gone through so much, and all you wanted was to be done with this and move on. But you couldn't. You couldn't because someone, someone who probably didn't even know your name and had absolutely nothing to gain by harming you, wouldn't let you.

The land was unfamiliar, perhaps a little frightening, but if nothing else, it was safe, far from the bombings and death that were already ravaging through your homeland and spreading farther every day. Those doing it weren't going to be stopped anytime soon.

Some of the people sitting next to you had already seen the worst of the worst, so far past any evil that an outsider could never comprehend it. Thousands of people had already been rounded up like animals and locked away. Those doing the imprisoning snidely referred to it as "protective custody," as insulting a term as could ever be used. Fellow passengers had informed you about what waited back home. They were called "camps" by those lucky enough to escape—and those sent there didn't leave.

Just over a year ago, hundreds had been in the very position you now found yourself. They had barely escaped the same enemy as you. They had spent weeks at sea, knowing they could start a new life. They'd sailed past these very lands, less than half a nautical mile from freedom.

And then they had been turned away. Ignored by some, like the president of this very country, and outright rejected by others, they'd been forced to turn around and go back to the very place they nearly died to escape from. Many of them were already dead and many more would be, very soon.

You had just barely escaped from your home, lucky enough to find a spot on this strange-looking ship and sail off to safety. The terrible weather, the horrible rations, the inescapable illnesses that plagued you and so many would be worth it if you could just make it over. But now, for the third time in less than a month, someone was making you wait. It was sad that you needed approval from anyone to do this, let alone someone with such an oppressive mindset, but it had happened before. Someone who thought it was fun to climb up on a pedestal and look down on you was doing so, just as the ones before had.

They didn't care. Or maybe, to give them the benefit of the doubt, they didn't realize how dangerous (in the extremely understated sense of the word) their refusal could be, what it could lead to for you, as it already had for so many in your homeland, and what it would, horrifyingly, mean to millions more.

But you did. You knew it all too well. Word about the unthinkable evil overtaking Germany had already started to spread throughout Europe, and this had become a case of getting out while you still could. If these people turned you away, as others had, literally, in the days before, you and so many others could soon be gone forever—and only because you'd committed the offense of practicing the "wrong" faith.

You'd hoped that a previous stop would be the last. You'd prayed that the one after that would be the end. Now there was this one, and based on what you'd heard from your fellow passengers and those on the outside, you wouldn't be here long. Once again, you'd be close enough to freedom to reach out and touch it, and someone else would yank it away, sending you back to a place that had almost meant your death to begin with.

It would take everything but a miracle to get you out of this. Several people who didn't know you, and who had plenty on their plates already, would have to donate time they didn't have, probably for compensation they wouldn't receive. Many around you had even taken the long shot of reaching out to someone who had an entire country to worry about but who might actually take the time to step in on behalf of a few dozen people she'd never met, let alone even been aware of.

It seemed impossible. You'd thought all was lost when you were forced to flee your homeland at high speed, but things were even more hopeless now. The first place your ship landed, only those with a few connections had been let off. You'd gone for another place, just knowing that someone there would have a heart.

You'd been disappointed again. Just like before, you'd been forced to watch others step off the ship and move on to safety while you were left behind. The ones stopping you weren't killing or even harming you themselves, but they were all too willing to stand around and let someone else do it. A few who were aware of the danger you faced refused to take a few small, harmless steps to prevent it. It makes one wonder who was actually worse.

As the minutes turned into hours, as the sun made its way across the sky, making things darker for you as if to mockingly represent one more loss, your time of death ticked closer. Torture and death were already rampant back in your homeland, and you were just one last refusal away from becoming the next victim.

And then, right out of nowhere, a glimmer of hope appeared.

WHEN THE PHONE RANG in their Newport News law office in early September 1940, the Morewitzes didn't realize how much history was on the other line. A friend of theirs was calling about a family he knew that had bought shipping tickets to Mexico and not been able to disembark. It was probably some misunderstanding, the Morewitzes thought. Maybe some bigot with too much power was throwing his weight around on them because of their faith or race or ethnicity. That was happening far too often, all around them. They'd seen bits and pieces from the newspaper about the *Quanza* matter as the ship had made its way up and down the coast, but such a matter seemed far from the level of finding a safe haven for someone whose life might depend on it.

But why not? Sallie Morewitz and her husband, Jacob, figured they'd sit down, argue with the opposing side for a bit, show a piece of evidence here

SS *Quanza* passengers and their friends and family on the dock below in Norfolk could only watch helplessly as their fate was decided elsewhere in Norfolk in September 1940. *Courtesy of Norfolk Public Library.*

and there and be done with it, a perfect way for a struggling law firm to make a few quick bucks. It would be one of the most common legal issues of its type in the legal community: lack of keeping one's word. Someone had drafted a contract. Someone else (maybe a few someones) had signed it. One had let the other down. Someone hadn't gotten what was agreed on. Yes, another breach-of-contract battle. These things can involve tons of money, but the type of case itself was nothing new.

Sallie and Jacob may have had more than enough on their hands already. Busy lawyers, especially in small firms, often do. In Virginia in 1940, a husband-and-wife legal team was a novelty almost big enough to divert the nearby James River down through the Carolinas. Many still considered the term *female lawyer* a hardcore oxymoron; it had been only a few decades since Congress had had the common decency to grant women the nationwide right to vote by handing the Constitution its Nineteenth Amendment. Sallie had made local history in 1933 when she became William & Mary's first lady from the law school to pass the bar. Not wanting to draw attention away from her husband's firm, she didn't spend much time in front of judges and juries, instead prepping her husband with briefs, research, deposition questions and all the other background work every law firm needs—a common practice for lawyers' wives nationwide at the time.

Now she and Jacob were trying to put together a future for themselves and their two sons in one of the legal world's least common practices. Maritime lawyers like the Morewitzes go to battle for fishermen, longshoremen, dockworkers and boaters, in matters involving everything from cruise ships to vessels to anything else designed to take one across one of the seven seas. It's not the most common type of legal practice, but Hampton Roads had long had a huge seafaring community—personal, professional, military, etc.—so these lawyers would have a place there as long as the Atlantic Ocean held out.

And there was something else about the Morewitzes, something that made them seem ominous to many and heroic to others: they were Jewish. That wasn't a very popular adjective in the 1930s; as Americans too commonly do, people did everything to shift blame onto the innocent. Still recovering from World War I and now in the midst of the Great Depression, Americans were poor and scared, with no one around to offer much in the way of inspiration; even exiting President Herbert Hoover admitted in March 1933, "We are at the end of our string. There is nothing more we can do."

Rather than get in gear and prove Hoover wrong—which America would eventually do, just not yet—it was simpler to find a minority group and hold it responsible for the misfortunes of the many. Many preached against the Jews for causing the First World War, and many witch hunters tried to hold them responsible for the Depression.

Some, however, had seen the Morewitzes as kindred. Poland would soon become the site of history's biggest atrocities, and the lawyers had helped many Jewish soldiers make it here from there, just as they had many faith-based allies from elsewhere in Europe. Before scoring his own legal degree from Richmond College (just before it morphed into Richmond University), Jacob had done his own fighting in the First World War, and he didn't want anyone in combat who didn't want or have to be there.

Literally a few days before this story begins, the Finnish ship *Edit H.* docked in Norfolk for fumigation; the entire crew was evacuated. Five Jewish soldiers had, very literally, sat down on the job, striking to avoid getting back on until work conditions improved. With the Morewitzes' help, the strike worked, and the ship left for Texas, the seamen joyfully and safely on land. It was cases like this that kept the Morewitz moniker in the spotlight of the local legal community. Money was never the family objective on rolling into court: they had enough of it (the Morewitzes already had a successful tugboat business and a beer distribution company), and they were well aware that much of their clientele didn't, sometimes allowing customers to pay them with slaughtered chickens.

World War II had begun the previous fall, and America was still teetering between the sides of the war. Would Old Glory become the newest Ally or the Fourth Axis? One newspaper after another reported on a fellow named Hitler and how he was leading Germany to one win after another in Europe, and no one, here or there, was sure what would happen next.

Americans didn't know what to believe. Some felt that Hitler and his friends had it right, and not just because they were drawing on the anti-Semitism that was still easy to find in America. Others feared that he—or Mussolini, Hirohito or another of their buddies—would get too powerful. They might upset one of Old Glory's friends, and we'd be forced into battle. Or, maybe worse, one of our friends might go turncoat and give them too much help. It was America and the Soviet Union at the top of the world superpower ranks, and the Russians were murmuring about just maybe joining the Axis themselves. If that happened, it would be do or die for the United States, and we'd just have to head over there and take care of business. But any Axis power having the brass to attack us personally? Of course not. We were too far away, geographically and politically, for that to ever happen. Right?

Jacob, a Baltimore native, had battled for the U.S. Navy years before. Then he and Sallie had set about repping those who had done the same. Soldiers from all over the world were looking for a way into America, and the two were hard at work looking for a way to help them. As they always did, the Morewitzes got rolling long before they met their new business partner. Sallie went to work on some drafts on contract breaches involving those on the sea. Jacob started rehearsing his arguments and client interviews. They'd been through this before and figured they'd be finished by the end of the week.

That September morning, just as he always did when there were cases to handle, Jacob rolled out of bed before sunrise. Just as she always did, Sallie had a hot breakfast ready, on her way to hold down the fort at the law office, ready to knock out those precious briefs and welcome more clients. One good luck kiss later, Jacob was on his way to work—and, as he'd find out very soon, straight into history.

CHAPTER 1

TRYING TO LEAVE

One girl had escaped from a concentration camp. She had fled toward France and undergone machine-gun attacks from swooping squadrons of German planes. She told of running to fall flat on her face, praying in ditches when the planes came over with their savage guns barking a death message. She finally made it to Lisbon, where she joined her brother, and they were furnished funds by relatives in Poland.

Several others had escaped concentration camps. One unfortunate family had first fled Czechoslovakia when Hitler invaded. They fled to Belgium, and it wasn't long until again the Nazi military machine was on their heels. From Belgium, they fled to France, and again they were set upon the road, fleeing for their lives. Automobiles in which they were traveling were subject to machine-gun attacks. Several persons on board the vessel were injured slightly during the attacks. Finally reaching the safety of Lisbon in Portugal, the refugees gathered all their available funds and chartered the Portuguese boat to bring them to Mexico, then expecting to find a haven.

—New York lawyer H.I. Fishbach,
who represented several* Quanza *passengers

One of the saddest statistics of World War II pertains to Poland's Jewish population. Before the war broke out, the Polish land boasted Eastern Europe's largest numbers of Jewish citizens: about three million. By the 1990s, that number had shrunk to fewer than four thousand, and it's only slightly higher today. Three million to four thousand: that's how strong and destructive the Nazi power was.

But long before the Nazis began to drop bombs and send stormtroopers to do their horrific work, many Jews could feel their dark power seeping into homes and homelands. As more and more of Europe fell under Hitler's spell, more and more began acting on it.

Just before the Second World War began, about seventy thousand Jews were living in Germany's eastern neighbor Belgium (of those, about twenty thousand had emigrated from Germany). Roughly half were in Antwerp, and nearly as many were about half an hour away in the capital, Brussels. In such proximity to the Nazi homeland, in a land with a close relationship with Israel, many Jews found themselves targets of Nazi harassment.

In school, recalls former resident of Belgium Malvina Parnes, "some of the kids knocked my head against the wall, and the teacher examined my head for lice. They said I was clean and well groomed for a Jewish child." Her nickname at school was *sale Juif*, French for "dirty Jew." Students refused to touch her, sit with her or even speak to her, and administrators did little about it.

"We led a comfortable and secure life at home, but school was terrible for me," she said. "Grade school was a terrible ordeal. I threw up every morning before going to school. The primary reason was my anxiety. I was surrounded by anti-Semitism in school, ranging from insults to physical abuse directed at me. My mother would come to school to speak to the teachers, but nothing changed."

When Itzak Rejdel's father was serving in the Polish army, he subtracted the *J* from his surname to conceal his faith. Later on, Itzak changed his own name to Irving. He was of the few family members to survive the Holocaust. "Life in Brussels was basically okay," Irving said. "There was some anti-Semitism, but we didn't really feel it. But when I was seventeen, my friends and I felt it was only a matter of time before this widespread hatred came to us in Belgium, too. We decided it was time to leave the country, believing that pro-Nazi sentiments would come to Belgium once more."

In the months after the war's beginning, more and more Jews in Belgium knew their lives were in danger, and they had nothing they could use to fight back. By late 1939, Malvina's father had set off for New York, hoping to establish a foothold in America in time for his family to follow. "It was the first time in my life I saw my father crying," she said. "He was trying to hide it from me, standing at a window. I remember it was December. It was winter, and he was standing there crying. I knew he was going so that we could eventually leave."

Ironically, in a sad way, her dad had already arranged for them to do so. The Parneses were set to sneak to Lisbon at the end of the month and board the liner *Serpa Pinto* to follow him to North America. But on the dawn of May 10, 1940, a tragedy took hold of Belgium that would not let go for years: the Battle of Belgium commenced. Just over two weeks later, Belgium gave in, and the Nazis all but owned the land. No one was leaving anytime soon. By the end of the war, almost half of Belgium's Jewish population would be killed.

"My anxieties were so great that I stayed out of school at every opportunity," said Malvina, who remembered watching from her Antwerp home as bombs fell on nearby Brussels. "I could not keep up with my studies, and this went on until Germany attacked Belgium, which in a way was merciful for me. I hate to say this. It saved me from a history exam—and, as it turned out, from going back to school." Also ironically, the *Pinto* would gain its own fame during the war, helping over 110,000 passengers escape, more than any other ship from Portugal. If its name is quietly ringing bells for other reasons, that may be because it's named after Alexandre Alberto da Rocha de Serpa Pinto, the Portuguese explorer who spent years exploring eastern Africa in the 1800s.

"My family had been living in Paris, and Germany before that," said Bob Miness, whose mother, uncle and grandmother were looking for an escape route. "They became French citizens in the 1930s, but they still had a house in Berlin."

On the very day that France fell, Miness's family drove across the border with Portugal. "They had been planning to leave for years," he explained, "but they didn't have the papers. They had to wait in Lisbon for the papers."

Many Jews packed up as much as they could in a short while. Knowing (and certainly hoping) that they'd be on a ship soon, many took only what they could carry by hand, not even what could fit in their cars. Several bundled up thousands of dollars of their life savings in bags and pockets and ran like hell. They rushed toward Portugal. Someone there might be willing and able to help.

Right around the war's beginning, Portuguese diplomat Aristides de Sousa Mendes openly defied the orders of his regime, issuing visas and passports to roughly thirty thousand refugees fleeing the Nazis. Portugal itself was neutral for much of the war, until the United States established a base there in 1944, but the nation enforced strict visa laws. Mendes went around the visa rules by first handing out the gifts and only then remembering to ask for required documentation. If refugees didn't have it on them, that was fine. They could just bring it by later (sure!).

Interestingly, while many elsewhere certainly were imprisoned and worse for such deeds, Mendes received only a one-year job suspension, during

As Nazi armies rolled through Europe, their victims could only flee in terror with what little they could carry. *Courtesy of Pauline Leger/*Nobody Wants Us *film.*

which he was paid. "If so many Jews are suffering because of one man, Hitler, surely I can suffer for so many Jews," said Mendes, who was later recognized by Israel as a Righteous Among the Nations and had a Portuguese monument named after him. "I do not have the right to let so many women, children and men die."

One lucky recipient was Salvador Dali, who escaped from France and, aboard the *Excambion*, followed a path similar to the *Quanza*'s, moving from Lisbon to New York and arriving in August 1940. Margret and H.A. Rey were both Jews who escaped Paris and, with Mendes's help, eventually made it to New York. Two years later, the pair published the first of the Curious George books, which still entertain young readers today.

A colleague of Mendes's wasn't so hospitable. A group of hopeful departers piled into a consul general's Lisbon office, certain he'd sign off on their visas and get them out and ready just as quickly as Mendes had. His boots on the table, the man just sat there, staring and nodding. Slowly, an evil grin started to stretch across his face. "Over my dead body," he vowed to the visitors, "will I allow any Jews into the United States." Fortunately, the group found someone else to approve their impromptu passports.

"Everything that we'd created and wanted to do had become nonsense," Irving Redel said. "It's very hard for someone to leave a lifetime of possessions and not come back. The Germans were advancing and we were running. We were leaving with the hopes that the British or the French would be able to counterattack, and somehow, we would be able to come back." Right around noon on June 25, he and his family left town. Before three o'clock that afternoon, the Nazis had closed the borders. The Rand family, whom we've already met and will meet again, escaped bombings by mere hours themselves.

As troops battled across not just Belgium but also the Netherlands, Luxembourg and other areas, roads became jammed with thousands of desperate escapees. Some hid from bombs under their cars and in ditches. Wrecked cars, broken wagons and even overflowing wheelbarrows and baby strollers littered the landscape.

Several members of the Parnes family were taken to a work camp. Malvina and her sister found themselves working mere yards away from their mother, who could only stare at them through a fence. Fortunately, it didn't last; their mother helped them escape, and an aunt charmed two young men into driving them part of the way. Some friendly nuns hid them at a farmer's house for a few days until everyone could escape toward Portugal.

It was there, however, that young Malvina had her closest brush with the war. As she stood near a farmhouse window, a bomb landed outside, just a few feet away. She froze in helplessness, certain that the next few seconds would be her last. But the bomb, happily, was a dud, and she managed to escape.

By early August, several hopeful departers had heard of the shipping company Companhia Nacional de Navegação, based in Lisbon. It wasn't known for passenger ships or cross-ocean journeys, but they didn't have time to be choosers. The company claimed it could get them to America safe and sound—well, if their funds were sufficient.

Simone Neufeld remembered walking into the shipping company office for a ticket. "The guy said, 'I'll take you, as long as you pay,'" she said. "We were bribing our way through. We had to pay for everything." The company, not even sure itself if the ship would make it back, forced passengers to purchase round-trip tickets, even knowing how many of them were praying it would be a one-way trip. It was just one more choice that had been stolen from them. But again, it was pay and leave or stay and die.

They needed to get away. Get somewhere, anywhere they could hide, isolate themselves from the bombs and guns and those who were using them. And everyone desperately tried to ignore the fact that, just over a year before, another group on the same trek hadn't been so fortunate.

CHAPTER 2

THE SS *ST. LOUIS* DISASTER

Take a moment to go back and read over the introduction at the beginning of this book. Reflect, once again, on what it would be like to rush from your war-torn homeland, driven out by those who would take your life without blinking and move on to violently take some more. And yet, if you managed to leave, you'd be luckier than many: auspicious enough to escape, to be one of nearly one thousand—no small number but miniscule compared to the number of those who were already lost or would be, all too soon—who found a spot on a ship that represented a voyage to freedom.

Isn't it interesting that a military action, no matter how deadly and destructive, transforms into an official "war" only when a few people sign a few documents? To those innocently caught in the middle of a battle, trench combat, hardcore bombing, rampant death and anything else that's basically a war without a declaration, the difference doesn't mean much. The papers that officially would deem Europe's battles "World War II" were still being edited, but war or no, Jews of the 1930s had become all too aware that an entire country—at least, its leading political party—had been openly calling for their destruction, imprisonment and death for years.

As it sadly became clear that the Nazis were an unstoppable force, at least then, hundreds of thousands of Jews fled Germany and Austria. The November 1938 horror of Kristallnacht was all the proof that 115,000 or more needed to escape, but over 30,000 were captured and imprisoned over those few precious days. After seeing much of their property destroyed and their friends and family jailed, deported or even worse, Jews knew they had to sacrifice what little they had to save anything at all.

At the docks of Hamburg, Germany's second-largest city behind Berlin, lay the key to freedom. The SS *St. Louis* had been crossing the ocean from continent to continent for years. While a few dozen German Jews who boarded the ship had long-held, legitimately obtained immigration visas, others had been forced to resort to more desperate means. Manuel Benitez Gonzalez, the Cuban immigration director, had been selling landing permits for about $160 each, which was serious money for anyone in 1939, especially those whose access to even their own funding had been stolen. Many, kept from withdrawing their money from German banks, had to reach overseas for financial help from their relatives.

On the night of May 13, 1939, the ship and its 937 passengers (some of whom had already spent time in concentration camps) pulled away from Hamburg. Gisela Feldman, who was still in high school back then, remembered sadly waving to those waiting back at the station. "We were the lucky ones," she recalled. "We managed to get out." Her father, along with dozens of her relatives, would be dead very shortly.

Trying to ignore the Nazi flag on the staff and the huge portrait of Hitler in the dining room, passengers made the best of things. They could dance and sing along with a band. They could swim in the pool. They could even watch movies in the small cinema, except, of course, on Fridays and Saturdays, when they were allowed to openly observe the Sabbath (one room was made into a synagogue), a privilege that had long been suppressed in Germany. Over the next few weeks, passengers could feel the ship getting closer to freedom, knot after knot. "We're going away," they assured each other and themselves. "We don't have to look over our shoulders anymore."

Onboard the ship were Moritz Weiler and his wife, Recha. Moritz's health had been deteriorating since before the ship launched. An available doctor did what he could, but Weiler passed away on May 23. A rabbi blessed the body, and Weiler received a sea burial that night. Just afterward, a depressed crew member threw himself overboard. The body wasn't recovered.

The harbingers of doom kept coming. Shortly after the deaths, Captain Gustav Schröder received a frightening telegram.

The Nazis had been ahead of them since the *St. Louis* left port. Propaganda had been one of the Nazi Party's most effective weapons in coming to power, and Holocaust champion Joseph Goebbels was using it at high volume. He'd already sent over a dozen Nazi agents to Cuba, spreading falsehoods about the *St. Louis* being loaded with criminals and fugitives who were there to corrupt Cuba, much as Germany already believed they would at home. They'd already inspired an anti-Semitic demonstration right there in Havana, and attendance had been huge.

Locals might not have needed much prodding to invent a problem with Jews, who numbered about five thousand in the Cuban capital. The Cuban government was listening: it passed a resolution basically revoking the passengers' visas. The more than nine hundred visas Gonzalez had sold were now deemed worthless. Only those who had obtained their travel papers—fewer than thirty passengers—would be allowed off the ship.

A telegram arrived informing Captain Schröder that the ship might not be able to land. He could read between those lines: there wasn't a chance in hell that Cuba was letting him in. Back in Germany, the Nazis had been blaring over the radio that the passengers had escaped with stolen money and jewelry.

Searching for a way around the decree and to land, Schröder and his crew fought to keep the news a secret. The passengers, seeing the coast of Florida and packed up and ready to depart, joyfully stood on deck, pointing out the Sunshine State's landmarks. Some sent telegrams to their friends and family, letting them know they'd be there soon. On the afternoon of May 26, those friends and family gathered at the Havana docks, waving and calling to their loved ones as the ship moved closer and closer. But when it stopped some distance from the docks, people started to worry.

Another telegram had arrived, ordering Schröder to stay some distance away. Police boats were sent out to ensure that no one tried to swim for shore. Cuban officials boarded the ship, their faces bearing the most disarming of smiles. They kept informing passengers that there had been just a few snafus. They'd be getting off tomorrow. Then the next day. Then the next day.

More and more days passed. Passengers began to fear the worst. For one man, it became too much. Already having been in the infamously pitch-black concentration camp Dachau, Max Loewe felt he had nothing left to lose, even with his wife and children onboard. On May 30, Loewe slit his wrists and jumped overboard. Batting at the water in a frenzy, Loewe clawed at his arms, trying to extend his wounds. A crew member leaped in after him, and Loewe was picked up and brought to a hospital. Six-year-old Gerald Granston was standing above, on deck. He would never forget witnessing Loewe's attempt at death. "If I close my eyes," Granston said, "I can still hear his shrieks and see the blood."

One suicide had been completed and another attempted. The situation was all but hopeless, and Schröder feared that more might take their own lives. It wouldn't have come as a complete surprise. Though a German himself, Schröder was no Nazi, and he knew quite well what would happen to his passengers (and, quite possibly, to him and his crew) if they fell back into the clutches of Hitler's strongmen.

The day after Loewe's attempt, the Cuban cabinet met, if only as a formality. The passengers weren't getting off. The *St. Louis* could leave on its own or be forced out by the Cuban navy.

"We always clung to the hope something was going to happen," said passenger Gerda Blachmann Wilchfort. "We thought, *They're not going to let us rot on the ocean.* I mean, something had to happen to us. Of course, the fear was that we would go back to Germany."

The Dominican Republic offered to allow the ship to land and then quickly rescinded its offer. Schröder sailed north, hoping that the United States would be more welcoming. "*America* was a magic word. It was the be-all and end-all," a passenger recalled. "We knew America would not let us down."

It did. Passengers cabled to President Roosevelt and Secretary of State Cordell Hull. Kids wrote letters to First Lady Eleanor. Nothing worked. America, citing its refugee quota, said no. By this point, such actions were popular among voters; polls at the time showed support for strong refugee restrictions. The U.S. military sent ships and planes to Miami to stop the *St. Louis* from landing. The Canadian prime minister messaged the ship to let it know not to bother showing up.

"We were not wanted," said *St. Louis* survivor Susan Schleger. "Abandoned by the world."

Schröder had no options left—except one. He'd sail back toward Hamburg. Then he'd make a quick switch, blast into the English coast and run his ship the hell aground. Then the passengers would have to be rescued. Before he could, however, one more cable arrived.

Back in America, news had already spread about the plight of the *St. Louis*, and people, including the Roosevelts, were trying to do at least something. American Jewish organizations were pressuring other countries to take the passengers in, and some were finally saying yes. Almost seven hundred of the passengers would get something of a safe haven.

The American Jewish Joint Distribution Committee pledged a cash bond of $500,000 (a whopping $11 million in today's dollars) to cover the relocation costs for those who found a place in Holland, France, England and, ironically, Belgium, where they were greeted with a new round of anti-Semitism (Loewe was given sanctuary in England). Later that month, the British ship *Orduna* and its seventy-two passengers were denied entrance to Cuba, but the ship was allowed to land in Panama and eventually let into the United States.

But many didn't survive. At least 250 people from the *St. Louis* were sent to concentration camps, and only a few would leave. Soon after, the trek came to be known as the Voyage of the Damned. If that sounds like the title of some redundant horror movie, we can only wish this were the case.

At the end of the day, government actions like this, done outside of Germany, though inadvertently, gave rise to Nazi idealism. As Hitler learned that Jews were being denied and sent away from other countries—on other continents that he barely communicated with, let alone controlled—he could keep sending the message to more and more followers: *Yes, we don't want Jews for these reasons. But don't just take our word for it—look how many other people feel the same way!*

For now, the *Quanza* folk could only pray they wouldn't be part of the next such chapter, but propaganda like that gets the public to listen, and the message was spreading right there in America.

CHAPTER 3

THE *QUANZA* SETS OFF

It was a sunny morning, on Aug. 8, 1940, when the Quanza *slowly sailed out of Lisbon Harbor. We remained a long time on deck, nostalgically watching the receding European coastline. When it had vanished altogether, we asked the purser to show us to our cabins.…So we spent our honeymoon in a cabin along with my parents, on a crowded refugee boat, rocking its way uncomfortably through the stormy Atlantic.*

***—Maria Bauer,* Beyond the Chestnut Trees**

Passengers poured onto the *Quanza*, in far too much of a hurry to consider much about their new carrier. It floated, it had a captain and crew and its company had agreed to take them across the ocean to freedom. That was all they needed. It was all they had time for.

But as she and hers speed-walked toward the boat, Malvina Parnes couldn't help but feel reality starting to shake what little reasons she had left to hope. "Walking down the steep hill to the dock, we saw the *Quanza*," she remembered, "and I thought to myself, *This little ship is going to take us all to America?*"

If passengers had been looking for something like the luxurious *Queen Elizabeth* or *Queen Mary*, the watershed cruise ships of the times, they weren't going to get it. But this was a case of taking whatever one had left to grab.

Following pages: The SS *Quanza*, normally a cargo ship based out of Portugal, suddenly became a passenger ship—and the last hope for hundreds trapped as World War II spread across Europe. *Courtesy of Norfolk Public Library.*

QUANZA
LISBOA
BALEIRA

The *Quanza* didn't look like a cruise ship simply because it wasn't. It was never intended to be. The vessel, built in Germany and launched as the *Portugal* by the Companhia Nacional de Navegação in 1929, was made to ship cargo of the nonliving kind. A rider from the past referred to it as a "passenger ship that took cargo," and that was probably a fairly common assessment. The ship, which received its new moniker a few months after going into service, had been carrying supplies back and forth from Lisbon to South Africa for some time and was occasionally sent down to South America. It could do that job exceptionally well.

While the *Quanza* weighed just over 6,600 tons, the *Elizabeth* and *Mary* were ten times that. While the Portuguese ship measured less than 420 feet long, *Mary* and *Elizabeth* were over 1,000. The *Quanza* rarely carried even 200 passengers, let alone the 336 who now rushed aboard it; the cruise ships could easily squeeze in over 2,000. And perhaps most damningly, *Elizabeth* had been crisscrossing the Atlantic Ocean every week for years, and *Mary* had done so several times. While the *Quanza* had quite a bit of shipping experience, this would be its maiden voyage from Europe to North America, and Lisbon to New York was a nearly 3,400-mile jaunt. Only a few days before, the ship had been yanked from "local" service and picked to jump across the ocean, its owners hoping that one of their most reliable would be lucky enough to make it over. But if it got in trouble, there would be little to do.

It had happened before. Less than two years after its launching, the *Quanza* nearly sank after colliding with a fellow cargo ship near Portugal. Much more recently—that very January, even—the ship was on its way home from Africa when a British warship stopped it in the high seas off Sierra Leone and removed two German sailors. Not long after, a French ship halted a different journey and removed some others.

"It was not a rowboat," asserted Wendy Juren of the Holocaust Commission of the United Jewish Federation of Tidewater. "It was a comfortable ship, and the way it became a refugee ship is that people were trying to get out, looking for ships that they could secure for refugees."

On August 9, over three hundred passengers watched their homeland get smaller and smaller as they finally set sail—or at least twin-screw propulsion. Some felt guilty that others couldn't be there with them, and they hoped their loved ones might find a spot on the next such journey. Some felt sadly acceptant about leaving their land, knowing that the tough decision was right, a shot at life instead of near-certain death and suffering. Others stood at the head of the ship, however few could fit there, staring at the seemingly endless dark blue sea that waved them toward freedom. Many more chose to stay belowdecks, trying to get used to the watery trip. Many had never even been on a boat, and now they'd be staying on one for at least a few weeks—maybe less, if they were lucky. This was their home now, and they were going to make the best of it. Part of that meant not thinking about the previous weeks and months.

"My sister was so seasick, she couldn't stand up," Parnes remembered. "No one could keep anything down." Piles of garbage would eventually weigh down the ship to dangerous levels.

A more helpless situation is tough to imagine. But very soon, the *Quanza* group would find themselves at the mercy of yet another antagonist, and no war weapon or place of hiding could protect them from this one.

CHAPTER 4

A NATURAL ENEMY

Several passengers tried to relax. It was finally time to head toward what they hoped would be the land of their freedom. The summer of 1940 was cooler than most, temperature-wise, but a steady, though not heavy, rainfall kept passengers off the decks for most of the journey. Several took advantage of the *Quanza*'s diverse food offerings. The crew had taken enough long trips to get familiar with keeping the ship's culinary supply strong for weeks at a time—or so they said.

"All we ate was sardines, sardines, sardines," said Eliza Weinman, who was on the ship as a teenager, "and then everyone got seasick." Jewish passengers were being forced to take their practice of kashrut to the extreme—and in some cases, even further. While the dietary tradition allows kosher foods such as fish to be consumed (unavoidable in this situation), they must be deeply cleaned beforehand (impossible in this situation).

Every day, Weinman's mom wore the same corset, hoping no one would notice the diamonds she'd sewn into it to hide them. Air issues on the ship would cause many of the passengers to develop pleurisy and other lung problems. "The ship was hot and smelly," said the youngest passenger, Annette Lachmann, herself the ripe age of three at the time. "I remember that, but I was glued to my mother the whole time. At least I had that. So now I think of those children down at the [U.S. southern] border being separated from their parents, from anyone they knew."

It was, claimed future Hollywood star Madeleine Lebeau, equivalent to being a "chicken in a cage."

Some read. Moms got mani-pedis in the makeshift salon, while their men played cards and listened to the ship's band. The kids played board games, hopscotch, anything they could do in a small area without making too much racket. Some even used the lifeboats for a private conversation, or even a tryst, once in a while.

Some passengers braved the precipitation long enough to step outside and hang out on the decks, waiting for that precious moment when they would see the welcome land of Ellis Island and that torch-bearing lady. Many had seen her in history books and magazines back home, and in those precious moments before they left, those back home in Europe had filled their heads with dreams of seeing her. The Statue of Liberty was the true physical depiction of Americana, and for most of them, it would be the first thing they'd ever see of their new home. Gold-paved streets were certain to be all around her.

"We slept in bunks in the ship's hold," remembered Malvina Parnes. "Eventually, they moved the four of us into a very small cabin, but I spent most of the voyage on deck. I was too seasick and unable to eat the awful food. We encountered enemy submarines, but they ignored us, fortunately."

Every sunrise would carry that fear. From the beginning of the war in August 1939 to July 1940, roughly five hundred ships had been torpedoed and sunk, so the *Quanza* folk knew they could be the next victims at any moment. Along with six ambulance drivers who had been released from concentration camps, two women who did similar jobs in France were on the *Quanza*, as were some sailors from the *Lucretia*, an unarmed Dutch oil tanker that had been sunk by a Nazi U-boat the previous July, an attack that killed two of their colleagues. A ship from Portugal, which was neutral in World War II, wouldn't automatically be seen as an enemy, but accidents happened, and there wasn't much to be done about it if one did. The Nazis weren't going to provide aid or take responsibility for such an error.

One day, some sharp-eyed passengers noticed a German submarine lurking nearby. Many froze. Others clasped hands and prayed. Some could only stare, not knowing if this was to be the last object they laid eyes on. But the submarine left, and they wouldn't see another for the rest of the trip.

Still, what if nature decided to step in, as it had a few decades before? Several passengers were old enough to recall the *Titanic* disaster of 1912, and while icebergs large enough to be dangerous are rare in the Atlantic in September, one the size of a small island had recently been reported not far off the coast of North Carolina.

Then, just two days after the ship departed from Lisbon, the clouds overhead suddenly got a little darker. And then heavier. More and more of them arrived. The waves around the *Quanza* began to grow and break against each other and against the ship. Sea voyages are always a little bumpy, but this was getting a little worse than that.

The rain increased on fast-forward. Thunder and lightning came along with it. Crew members started to bring chairs and other objects inside from the decks. Other officials were trying to power their ship through and around the storm without getting too far off course.

Things got worse and kept doing so. It was clear that this was no regular thunderstorm. Storms near Portugal's islands had become a regular enemy for the *Quanza*, but this was something new, something longer, something more dangerous.

People over in America had recently seen America's dark side, several times over. The 1940 hurricane season had been relatively calm for the first few months, but nature had been showing its destructive side since the start of August. In the first week of the month, a hurricane had dumped over three feet of rain in Louisiana, more than the state had ever seen. About $11 million in damage had been done, and seven people died. But before that squall even ended, another was located far south. This was the one coming for the *Quanza* folk.

The hurricane, which eventually moved all the way up to a Category 5 (such storms weren't being officially named at the time), landed in South Carolina on August 11 and then spent the next few days wreaking havoc all over the Southeast. Hundred-mile-per-hour winds and several feet of rain moved as far inward as Kentucky and north up to Maryland. By the time the storm, one of the worst of the century, had dissipated, fifty people were dead and $13 million in damage had been done.

Aboard the ship, crew members rushed around the decks, shoving lifejackets into people's hands and all but yanking passengers inside. Those up at the helm stayed there and could do little but hope and pray. They knew that if the passengers saw those in charge panicking, the entire ship could descend into chaos.

"The waves and troughs were immense," Parnes said. "All passengers were given life preservers and moved to the top deck." The passengers couldn't believe it. They might have escaped death by days or even hours back in Europe. At any time, an enemy ship or submarine could mistake them for a hostile visitor and torpedo them to the sea floor. Now Mother Nature was adding herself to their enemy list.

Day after day, although the storm sometimes made it difficult to tell midnight from noon outside, the passengers huddled together. Parents kept telling their children that things would be okay soon, that this ship would do just fine against this mess. Others tried to send messages to their families in case things didn't end well. But as the storm turned west and went farther inland, it finally moved away from the *Quanza* and weakened. The rain slackened, although it never went away. Passengers went back to the rail, armed with binoculars and the occasional telescope, desperately hoping that that welcome land would one day, one hour, come into view.

Then came the morning of August 19, when the sunrise illuminated something beyond the wavy blueish-ness. They could see something else. It was green. It was brown. It was gray. It was land. Finally, their new home was there for the entering. The war back at home and the troubles they'd faced along the way were finally over. The most difficult journey they'd ever take showed a clear finish line.

"This part of the trip was much gentler," Parnes said. "We were always within sight of the United States coastline, the sea was calm and the crew put up a makeshift swimming pool." Steadily, the group at the rail grew. Feelings of joy and relief rushed through the crowd. Just a few more knots, and they'd be free. Maybe they'd run right off, find a nice hotel and lie around for a few days. After spending weeks without solid ground and a comfortable bed, that would be heavenly. Maybe they'd celebrate their status as America's newest additions by visiting Ellis Island, where so many newcomers had landed before.

Cheers and sighs could be heard all over the ship. Random hugs were handed out here and there and everywhere. As New York City drew closer, passengers packed up their bags. No one had had the time or the space to carry much, and many belongings had been lost since shipping off back at Lisbon. But no matter how little anyone had, it would be enough.

The *Quanza* made it to within a few meters of New York Harbor. As it slowed more and more, passengers lined up on deck, barely able to keep themselves from leaping over the guardrails onto land. Even though they were a few hours north of the nation's capital, they couldn't think of a more American place to land. The toughest journey most of them had ever taken was at an end.

But then, as they were about to heartbreakingly find out, it wasn't.

CHAPTER 5

BANNED FROM NEW YORK

They looked out at abandoned buildings. They saw the homeless, stretched out up and down the sidewalks, forced to battle New York's legendary summer heat from the outside looking in, having no place to live, work or even stay for a few short days. Things weren't quite as bad as in previous years, when the Great Depression held the nation in a powerful grip of despair, but recovery was still far away.

And it could have been mistaken for heaven. No wars. No bombing. No enemies looking for prisoners. As the *Quanza* passengers watched their ship sputter slowly toward Brooklyn's Hamilton Avenue at Pier 35, they felt relief, joy and, for the first time in weeks, even months, hope.

Yes, they were stepping onto a new continent with little to start out with, but they knew they'd see tonight, let alone tomorrow. Most had only heard of America, never ventured anywhere near it, but now it was the most welcome sight. From far away, they could see the Empire State Building. No other structure in the world stood higher. But a little bit closer, a little bit smaller, stood the true emblem of Americana itself, the lady hoisting a torch into the air as a sign of welcome, imploring nations across the world, "Give me your tired, your poor, / Your huddled masses yearning to breathe free, / The wretched refuse of your teeming shore. / Send these, the homeless, tempest-tost to me, / I lift my lamp beside the golden door!"

Sixty years before, Emma Lazarus had written those words as part of her sonnet "The New Colossus" to raise funds for construction of the statue. Throughout the late 1880s, Lazarus was heavily involved in helping refugees escape to New York from European anti-Semitism. Lazarus, who, sadly, wouldn't live to see her words inscribed on Lady Liberty's pedestal in 1903, could feel their suffering; she herself was an American Jew.

Perhaps the newcomers could learn a thing or three about Americana in a show at Radio City Music Hall. They could use, and had certainly earned, a few days of rest and relaxation at Coney Island or the New York World's Fair, whose theme song proclaimed, "Better times, here to stay, as we live and laugh the American way." One woman all but groveled for a trip to the local salon, being "desperate to have her hair coiffed." Or maybe they'd just charge off the ship, find the nearest bus and bolt off to their relatives and a new life. Who knew? Who minded? All that mattered was that they were safe, from war and nature at sea, and would stay that way for a long time.

Just the month before, a ship was leaving New York for Europe when a group of frightened anti-Nazis leapt overboard and attempted to swim for shore. The U.S. Coast Guard picked them up and gave them a place to stay on Ellis Island. The *Quanza* group hoped to meet these people.

As the sun rose that August 20, tugboats pulled up on all sides of the ship, and the passengers just knew they were there to escort them to safety. No more endless cans of sardines to chow upon; by noon, they'd be enjoying a kosher meal in the huge ballroom of nearby Asti's, which millions of viewers would see decades later in 1988's blockbuster Tom Hanks comedy *Big*.

Lined up on the *Quanza*'s deck, passengers watched one group of riders after another stroll off the ship and onto solid ground. Paul Brooks, Robert Carson and the rest of the six ambulance drivers who'd spent frightening time in concentration camps were released. So were dozens of other passengers.

Surrounded by others on the ship, Simone Neufeld and her family waited their turn. "We stood there and watched them get off," she remembered. "We desperately wondered why no one would tell us."

Anxiously waiting on the dock, Malvina's father stared at his family, feeling his long-held state of glumness starting to lift. He'd been in New York since the year before, but that feeling of emptiness wouldn't go away until everyone else was there with him. His wife, her sister and his daughters knew they'd be in his arms soon. While they, and so many others, were desperate to get off the ship, he was just as eager to get on, if only for a moment.

And then, there he was. Malvina ran to her dad, drowning him in hugs, kisses and tears of joy. He handed her new clothes to wear and food to eat. Everyone gushed about how close they were to being back together. Then the guards came back. Her father was being removed from the ship—alone.

America was becoming the *Quanza*'s next victimizer. Nationwide fear and anti-Semitism were too strong to let more than a few off. Only those with some name recognition—like the ambulance drivers—or those who could convince certain people that their visas were legitimate were being allowed off. The rest, handicapped by (often McCarthy-esque) accusations that their travel documents were forged, invalid or otherwise unacceptable, were staying right where they were. Government officials had issued an order saying that no one else was coming ashore.

This was a case of guilty until proven innocent, and the passengers, although many of them were wealthy, had little more than their words to prove their intent. Perhaps guardsmen on the shore saw many upper-class possessions and assumed that one could only obtain such things through compensation that, while generous, was coming from those of the darkest (as in illegal) means. Maybe these people had been paid well for harming others and were looking to do so again.

"Nobody wanted us," remembered Neufeld, who was among the dozens of passengers held onboard, mere feet from freedom. Over 120 others thought the same. A sense of hopelessness as ominous as the midnight sea, perhaps even bigger than when they left Lisbon, overtook the ship as Captain A. Herberts and the crew steered the ship back out to sea.

Malvina Parnes's father and so many other friends and family of the unlucky could only stand and watch while their spouses, children, parents and everyone else sailed off into the morning. Many passengers went back to their makeshift cabins and collapsed; surely, they thought, they were done for. Malvina paced all over the *Quanza*, her hands acting out an imaginary piano recital to give her some sort of focus, any aspect of control in the grip of helplessness.

The *Quanza* was now headed south, its next destination Veracruz, on the eastern coast of Mexico. Over the coming decades, it would become one of the country's most popular tourist attractions. For the *Quanza*'s passengers, it represented their last hope.

CHAPTER 6

ACTRESS

Still, it wasn't all bad for the passengers, especially not the fellows. For a few moments, the *Quanza*'s crew could hope, they'd be lucky enough to encounter the most welcome of distractions.

Almost half the *Quanza*'s passengers were adult males, and there were a few teenagers creeping around the ship as well. And for a few brief moments, a lovely sight onboard could take certain minds off the troubles ahead and past. When this beauty happened to casually stroll by, the *Quanza*'s pseudo-machismo levels shot skyward to the point that the ship seemed to gain weight.

They could have sworn they'd seen her before. Maybe they passed her on the street on the way to Lisbon. Or maybe, if only for a few seconds, she'd already been on the big screen back in her French homeland. And once she got to North America, Madeleine Lebeau would be there again.

By early 1943, America didn't need any new reasons to stand up and face down anything with a German connection. The war was on. It had been for over three years, and it would stay that way for two more. That Hitler guy needed stopping, and young men across America, and much of the globe, dreamed of being the one to put a bullet between his eyes.

Hollywood had long since jumped into the cultural battle. The month after the *Quanza* issue, none other than Charlie Chaplin satirized the hell out of Adolf himself in *The Dictator*, which would outearn any of his Tramp films. Frank Capra, fresh off *Mr. Smith Goes to Washington* and years from *It's a Wonderful Life*, had literally shown Americans the importance of the war effort in the *Why We Fight* propaganda film series, among several flicks like them he'd put together during the decade.

After four Best Director nominations in the 1930s and '40s, Michael Curtiz saw a new shot to finally grab his statuette. As film fans took to war pictures, Curtiz happened upon the unpublished play *Everybody Comes to Rick's*, which looked to him like it could make it from the stage to the big screen. War and unrequited love have laid the groundwork for so many tales of every type; here, he could work with both at once.

Rick's bar had become a place where literally everyone came, from refugees looking to make the same trip as the *Quanza* to those who were imprisoning their friends and families back in Germany. Soldiers who might be trying to blow each other away the very next day could sit there and guess how many francs the guy across the table would raise them before, hopefully, folding. The proprietor, Rick, wasn't much good at being noble: drinking all the time, casting out a lady who truly cared for him, all in the sad name of unrequited love. Then, out of all the gin joints in the world, into his walked the original object of his affection.

Murmurings about the film had been leaking out of New York since it premiered there on Thanksgiving 1942. The following January, filmgoers around the world got to visit a large Moroccan city: *Casablanca*. Lebeau didn't get much screen time in the film, which overcame iffy reviews and unspectacular opening box-office receipts (though it was much more successful than an absolute flop the previous year called *Citizen Kane*) to reach the level of legendary in the coming years. Lebeau's Yvonne is the very woman scorned by Bogie's Rick early on before some past beauty called Ilsa arrives. As the film winds down, however, she gets her standout moment. And she'd had some sad preparation.

The men on the *Quanza* were right: they actually had seen this lady in the movies—if, of course, they had some pretty sharp eyes. Madeleine Lebeau had been in the background of 1939's *Girls in Distress*, but she didn't even get her name in the credits. Later that year, the teenager, who'd been studying acting since grade school, married Marcel Dalio, who'd just appeared in the masterpiece *Grand Illusion*. She was his second wife, and he was nearly a quarter-century older than her. That's probably why, when the *Quanza* crew was gawking at the bombshell, it may have been easy for eager onlookers to brush him aside. Maybe they truly thought he was her dad. In typical hormone-based loudmouth mode, one teenager bragged to anyone who would listen that he'd shared a secret tryst with her, one that she'd been intimating since the ship left port. It will never be known if that was true.

Still, by that point, Lebeau and Dalio had already been through their own horror movie. He had already lost several family members to the Nazis and would never see many more again. They had managed to escape Paris just before the Germans stole it, barely making it to the Spanish border with a nice car, a little jewelry and a few thousand dollars. That's where authorities kept them in a hotel room for two months. "I told them I wanted to go to the U.S., but I had no American visa," Lebeau remembered. "I figured that once in Chile, I could eventually get to America."

Someone offered her such a visa. All it would cost was her fancy car and her jewelry. With no other option, she gave them up. They barely made it to Lisbon, where seats on the *Quanza* cost them another $2,000. At the first few stops, Lebeau was accused of having a false passport and nearly taken off the ship by the wrong people. Local Veracruz authorities informed her that her passport was an out-and-out forgery. But Lebeau and Dalio managed to stay aboard the *Quanza* and as safe as anyone there could profess to be.

"The people on the boat are really prominent persons, [such as] Monsieur and Madame Dalio," said Rabbi Stephen Wise, in perhaps a bit of an overstatement, considering Lebeau had hardly made her mark back in France, "whose fame in France is on par with that of the Barrymore family in America."

In the past decade alone, Lionel Barrymore had starred in Best Picture winners *Grand Hotel* and *You Can't Take It With You* and won an acting Oscar for *A Free Soul*, and his sister Ethel was in and out of the acting spotlight for decades, finally scoring her own Oscar for 1944's *None but the Lonely Heart*. But it was their brother John who would become one of the first ever to be labeled a matinee idol, playing Dr. Jekyll, Mr. Hyde, Captain Ahab, Sherlock Holmes and Don Juan in the 1920s alone and then continuing as a household name into the next decade, including an appearance alongside his brother in *Grand Hotel*. The year before the *Quanza* issue, he starred in the smash comedy *Midnight*, though his hard living (and drinking) ways caught up to him shortly thereafter and ended his life in 1942. Now, decades later, his granddaughter Drew carries on the family's acting trend.

Lebeau and Dalio, who had worked with the passengers to improve their English during the trip, eventually made it off the ship, up to Canada and then back to Hollywood. A year and a half later, the pair appeared mainly in the background of a film that was to become a household name.

In *Casablanca*, Lebeau's (sadly soon-to-be-ex) husband plays an uncredited croupier who congratulates card game champions, and Lebeau is Yvonne, the former hopeful paramour of Humphrey Bogart's Rick Blaine. After a one-night stand and way too much booze, he keeps blowing her off—typical male. When Yvonne shows back up near the end, she's accompanied by a German soldier. Ironically, many of the film's German cast members were actually Jewish and/or refugees, much like Lebeau herself.

While Rick is upstairs discussing a business deal, a strange sound comes from below. It's "The Watch on the Rhine," one of the many unofficial German national anthems of the time. The tune had spurred *All Quiet on the Western Front* to winning Best Picture in 1930, but here, its impact is different. As a group of soldiers and a few customers join in, Rick storms right the hell over. His band's going to play "La Marseillaise," France's own "Star-Spangled Banner," and he's going to be in the vocal lead.

But not solo, or not for long. Patrons quickly leap to their feet, becoming an impromptu chorus. We see Yvonne—but maybe a little more so, during her closeups, we see Lebeau. We hear her voice above others'. We see tears pour down her face. She might just have been flashing back to her *Quanza* days—or, actually, her pre-sailing days back in Paris.

Their voices overtake the Germans', and applause rises almost as loud. It's obviously not as famous as "Here's looking at you, kid" or even "We'll always have Paris," as few scenes in world cinematic history are, but many today refer to the scene as one of the most patriotic—especially for a French song rendition—in film history.

CHAPTER 7

MEXICO SAYS NO

It was over for them. Parnes and the others would never see their loved ones again. All that effort, all that luck, all that courage, all that money spent would be for nothing.

The ship had arrived in Veracruz on August 30, and passengers had started to disembark. A dozen stepped off, then a dozen more. But as the number of departers reached close to forty, said one passenger, "something suddenly went wrong."

As the *Quanza* passengers showed the transit visas they had received from the Mexican consul back in Lisbon, Mexican officials suddenly decided, off the cuff, that the consul didn't have the authority to grant such documents. Not required to substantiate their decision, they denied the visa, and passengers were turned right around.

On the first Thursday in September 1940, an order arrived at the *Quanza*. This one could overrule any other in a moment. President Lázaro Cárdenas was personally ordering the ship back to sea. Even if every other person in Veracruz—hell, just about all of Mexico—wanted them to stay, this statement was stronger than all. Just as had been the case in New York, Cárdenas feared that some anti-Americans were among the *Quanza* group, and he had decided to err on the side of obvious caution, denying the good guys to weed out the villains, real or otherwise.

Mexico was fresh off a civil war, its economy wasn't doing well and Cárdenas's labor leaders pressured the government to restrict Jewish and Chinese immigration. Berlin had sent some Nazi leaders to hold anti-Jew rallies, and anti-Semitism was growing as well. Also, as petty as it may sound, Cárdenas was three months away from the end of his term, and he might not have wanted to get involved in—or had the power to fight—this new battle. Ironically, the former general came back as the country's minister of war two years later to help Mexico through World War II, establishing a close alliance with America along the way.

New York lawyer H.I. Fishbach, who'd already been contacted by some *Quanza* passengers, had gone down to Veracruz to see about getting them on land. It hadn't worked out. "We people in America should prepare ourselves for what may come," Fishbach remarked. "If we can't see the handwriting on the wall and maintain our precious liberties, then we are not entitled to these things which we hold so dear."

Mexico had just ended up as a replay of New York. The *Quanza* group had sailed into Veracruz full of high hopes and gotten to within inches of freedom, only to be turned away again. Once again, the ship went sailing out—and this time, there was nowhere else to go. They'd run out of chances in North America. There were no more stops to make, nowhere to go except back to the land they'd given up everything to escape. Escorted out by Mexican gunboats, the group felt more hopeless than ever.

"There was a momentary ray of light," one passenger wrote in a letter, "and everything turned dark again....I don't want to lose my courage no matter what—I don't want to give up....We are very desperate. Now we have a new trouble—we don't know how we will be received in Lisbon because we no longer have entry visas."

> *For them, this situation is a living hell on earth. Their hopes get lower every day.*
>
> —*Stephen Wise*

Here's where Stephen Wise steps into our story. His importance will grow at high speed over the following pages.

Wise was a founder of many Jewish causes and a member of even more. His leadership as one of the Jewish community's most well-known rabbis had won him favor in politics, and he was a liaison to President Wilson and an advisor to Roosevelt. Wise was one of the first to urge Roosevelt to stand against the Nazi regime, and he attempted to stage a boycott of German products and services as early as 1933; four years later, Madison Square Garden held a full-blown "Boycott Nazi Germany" rally. As Nazi rule grew stronger overseas and started to show influence in America, Wise helped create the World Jewish Congress in Switzerland in 1936. Decades later, the group still battles anti-Semitism and has offices all over the world, with its headquarters in New York City.

Like many Americans, Wise had become all too aware of the *Quanza*'s plight. But unlike most, he personally knew that Roosevelt wasn't ready to show his charitable side in the matter. At the Havana Conference the previous July, ministers of foreign affairs from around the world—except those who expected to side with the Axis—joined to vow that an attack on any would be defended against by all. However, the participating countries also decided to take extra steps against allowing in refugees from countries they didn't trust. Handing out fake or invalid visas was encouraged, as was the creation of blockades to let newcomers know they weren't welcome. U.S. Secretary of State Cordell Hull represented America at the Cuban event and spoke as loudly as any in favor of the makeshift border closures.

A quarter-century before, Wise had worked with Secretary of the Navy Josephus Daniels to spare some battleship space to send food to Palestine during the First World War. Now Daniels was the U.S. ambassador to Mexico. Considering Daniels's outspoken white supremacist and pro-segregation views, it seems strange that he would be close friends with Wise, who was not only Jewish but had also helped found the NAACP in 1914. But he was, and if the *Quanza* matter was important to Wise, Daniels felt he owed it to his pal and the passengers to look into it. However, he admitted in a letter to Wise just before the *Quanza* left Mexico, "I took matter up with authorities but could do nothing. They are adamant. Ship with passengers has gone to Nicaragua where it is reported but not officially that passengers will be received."

Wise had no reason to question Daniels's honesty, as the Mexican government had already messaged Nicaragua that the *Quanza* was coming its way. Sadly, Wise was also aware of how close the passengers had come to freedom before and that nothing was for certain. "The State Department and Department of Justice are going to be as helpful as it will be possible," he told Daniels hopefully. "I rather think they may let most of those people come in as persons who are in danger because they are refugees from Belgium, to which country as one-time Germans or Poles they cannot return."

Passengers pleaded to have the ship diverted to Nicaragua or to the *Quanza*'s familiar shipping grounds back near Portugal. Some even begged the crew and the captain to just brush *this close* to Florida; they were willing to strap on lifejackets and swim gear and freestyle their own way to shore. Captain Herberts scoffed and went straight to work. He was going to go back across the ocean and be done with this. Passengers could only stare forlornly at the waves, knowing this might well be the last month they'd ever see.

"All sorts of excuses were made," remembered Malvina Parnes. "I was old enough to understand the danger we were in, just looking at my mother and my aunt, and I knew we were in desperate trouble. We were going back to Europe and the war."

But there was just one problem for Herberts: his small (by steamship standards) ship didn't have enough fuel to get all the way across the Pacific. Not anticipating the jump from New York to Mexico, the crew hadn't loaded enough coal to get back—not yet. There had to be one more stop in North America.

When passengers learned that the city of Norfolk, Virginia, could be their only lifeline, the ship's telegraphing station went up like a firework. Wise himself, not ready to give up, was already on his way north, hoping to get to Virginia in time to convince a few others to help.

Many passengers contacted friends and family in America, imploring them to visit Old Glory's Old Dominion. Some reached out to local and national organizations that helped refugees and other (hopeful) Jewish visitors. And yes, many started calling lawyers. Surely there was something that could be done about this in the court system. Others tried to get in touch with the State Department.

Mortiz Rand, aboard the *Quanza* with his family, messaged his old pal Ralph Josephson in Hampton Roads. Josephson himself hadn't practiced maritime law for some time, but Rand thought he might have some old contacts in the area. Josephson did. He picked up the phone, dialed the Morewitzes' office and set the plans in motion for a shot in the dark that might just enlighten everything.

While Rand was banging out his message to Josephson, a large group of female passengers gathered in a room nearby. After expecting and experiencing the worst for so long, they felt they had nothing to lose. So they went higher: higher up the East Coast from Florida, Virginia and Washington, D.C., to a higher power, at least in name, than anyone else their colleagues were considering, a bigger public figure than anyone in Virginia, almost anyone in America, just about anyone in the entire world.

CHAPTER 8

ELEANOR ROOSEVELT STEPS IN

Today—and probably for generations to come—Eleanor Roosevelt stands above almost all in the ranks of First Ladies determined to be known for more than being married to the president. While most presidents' wives have chosen to stay in the background and maintain whatever privacy someone as prominent as a First Lady can be afforded, Eleanor was having none of that.

Before her husband was even governor of New York, let alone president, Eleanor was a leading voice in favor of women's voting rights during the 1920s (when Franklin did run in 1928, more members of the public recognized his wife than they did him). She played a strong role as he formed his cabinet in 1932 and rearranged it as his administration continued. Eleanor helped him finalize the New Deal, which established a set of reforms, projects and programs that gradually lifted America out of the Depression. At that time, she was all over America, letting victims know that her husband felt their pain and was doing what he could to make things better. She championed equality for minorities and women in ways that few in politics, regardless of gender or position, ever had before.

Again, this was a choice, not a requirement. Most First Ladies make the decision to stay in the background. Eleanor simply decided to be her own person, not just Mrs. Roosevelt. That doesn't necessarily make her better than her fellow First Ladies, just more well known.

But like everyone else, Eleanor had a past. And like everyone else, her past had a few notable mishaps and mistakes. Had the *Quanza* matter happened a few years earlier, Eleanor might not have gotten involved at all, let alone to the extent she did. Certain mindsets that were stuck in the minds of too many influenced her for a time. After a 1918 fundraiser for Bernard Baruch, who was then an advisor to President Wilson and would later hold such a position in the Roosevelt administration, Eleanor declared to her mother-in-law that "the Jew party [was] appalling." Ironically, though Baruch was himself Jewish, his father was in the Ku Klux Klan.

Even after Kristallnacht caused a (temporary) wave of sympathy toward Jews around the world, Eleanor opined, "I think it is important in this country that the Jews as Jews remain unaggressive and stress the fact that they are Americans first and above everything else…and, as far as possible, wipe out in their own consciousness any feeling of difference by joining in all that is being done by Americans."

The very next year, discussing the Todhunter School, a private New York City academy for women, Eleanor said,

> *I'm very sorry, but I'm afraid there's a feeling, even, I think, among the Jews themselves, that the spirit of the school, and the school itself, would be different if we had too large a proportion of Jewish children.…The difficulty is that the country is still full of immigrant Jews, very unlike ourselves. I don't blame them for being as they are. I know what they've been through in other lands, and I'm glad they have freedom at last, and I hope they'll have the chance, among us, to develop all there is in them. But it takes a little time for Americans to be made. And, meanwhile, the old stock can't feel they're Americans, and unfortunately, they also class real Americans who are Jews together with them. Well, one day, I hope, we'll all be Americans together.*

By the time her husband grabbed the White House, however, Eleanor's views had opened and softened. Her friend Dr. Alice Hamilton, who became Harvard's first-ever female faculty member in 1919, spent a few months in Nazi Germany in 1933, and she and Eleanor sat down with Franklin immediately afterward to discuss what life was like for the victimized there, but he did little with the information.

That pattern was repeated in February 1939, just a few months before the SS *St. Louis* shipped off to nowhere. Democrat Robert Wagner of New York and Massachusetts Republican Edith Nourse Rogers attempted to get a bill through Congress to expand the existing quota laws and allow ten thousand Germans under age fourteen into America in each of the next two years. Eleanor tossed her support behind the bill, the first legislation she supported as First Lady. But her husband, who never even commented on it, decided to listen to the overwhelming anti-immigration mindset of the time, and the bill never even got to a vote.

In the summer of 1940, Eleanor cofounded the U.S. Committee for the Care of European Children to help bring Jewish refugee children to America. She was working with the newly founded Emergency Rescue Committee, which helped evacuate artists, authors, scholars, politicians, labor leaders and other prominent citizens from German-occupied France. She persuaded her husband to authorize over five hundred emergency visas for those trapped there. She also worked with an organization called Hadassah (named after Esther of the Book of Esther, a heroine of the Hebrew Bible) to help Jews immigrate to Palestine.

On September 10, 1940, Eleanor and Franklin were on a jaunt to his boyhood home, Hyde Park, in southeastern New York. Suddenly, a messenger showed up with a letter for Eleanor. This one was different, he claimed. It wasn't from a friend from the political world, and it wasn't a piece of admiration from someone who, like so many young women in America, dreamed of being a lady just like Eleanor when she grew up. It wasn't from someone with a story idea for the multiple newspaper and magazine columns that carried her name on the byline (Eleanor had recently written a few such articles in support of opening her country's immigration doors a little wider).

This was something else, and she could tell from the return spot on the envelope. Eleanor quickly opened it. The next few moments, and words, would change everyone and everything very quickly. "Eight war refugees, steamer Quanza, threatened transportation back Europe because Mexico disclaimed transit visas," it cried. "Implore help. Steamer stopping Norfolk Wednesday. Beg possibility landing."

Eleanor Roosevelt's efforts on behalf of war refugees like the SS *Quanza* passengers have won her a place as one of American history's highest-regarded First Ladies. *Library of Congress.*

"Women Passengers"

Per usual for Eleanor, she went straight into campaign mode. This time, she had a small audience. She insisted to Franklin that these people weren't here to spy for the Nazis or the Communists, hoping she was right. They could be future patriots if they just got a chance. They could make a great difference in this country. All they needed was a little help, as long as it was coming from someone with some pretty solid power.

Just over a year before, she'd seen her husband, and far too many others, adopt a position of inactivity as the *St. Louis* was refused permission to dock in Florida and was forced back to Europe, sending hundreds to their deaths in the Holocaust. That wasn't going to happen this time. If Eleanor still had the slightest shred of anti-Semitism within her (and there's nothing to indicate that she did, nor had she for several years), the previous disaster had erased it for good, and now she and her husband could make up for lost lives.

"Even the silence of the American Jewish community was beyond unfortunate, disgusting perhaps," explains Eleanor expert Blanche Wiesen Cook. "Eleanor Roosevelt acted as a visionary, saying, *We will have peace when we all have education, jobs, housing, security and health care*. She made the refugees an interest, opposed fascism and said that everybody on the SS *Quanza* could be her guest."

Facing an upcoming election and mindful of his country's anti-immigration mindset, Roosevelt, despite strong support from the Jewish community in his first few elections, chose to drag his wheelchair wheels. Eleanor turned to her supporters. She sent a cable to the State Department, pleading for someone to do something, anything. She sought to get Breckinridge Long on her side. Not surprisingly, it didn't work. Long hardly paid attention to the message. He'd helped turn refugees away before and would again, now and the next time some outlanders tried to sneak by. He was sure that others in the department felt the same way.

Except, as he would sadly and the *Quanza* folk would joyfully learn over the next few days, they didn't.

CHAPTER 9

BRECKINRIDGE LONG

[Franklin] *Roosevelt took this "I'm not going to get involved" attitude and put the responsibility on Breckinridge Long. He was more concerned about the votes, which is typical politics. It's disturbing how anti-Semitic Breckinridge Long was, with his "America First!" mentality.*

—Filmmaker Laura Seltzer-Duny

Breckinridge Long's motives in the *Quanza* matter will always be a matter of debate. Some label him a full anti-Semite, which he denied. Others defend him (up to a point) by claiming he didn't have an issue with the Jewish population specifically but rather wanted to close America's borders—as much as he had the authority to do—to virtually everyone, protecting Old Glory against potential spies and invaders. The truth will never be fully known. However, during his time as FDR's ambassador to Italy, Long called the Mussolini regime "the most interesting experiment in government to come above the horizon since the formulation of our Constitution." And if that wasn't enough to show his motives, in 1938, Long scribbled in his diary an impromptu book review, calling the book he'd just read "eloquent in opposition to Jewry and to Jews as exponents of Communism and chaos."

The object of his praise? None other than *Mein Kampf*. "My estimate of Hitler as a man rises with the reading of his book," Long continued.

It's a sad fact that Long was responsible, intentionally or otherwise, for the deaths (and certain near-deaths) of many who deserved to live and would have, if a few decisions had been changed—or, in some cases, never had to be made at all.

Just a few months after Roosevelt appointed him assistant secretary of state in January 1940, Long sent out a memo to his colleagues asserting, "We can delay and effectively stop for a temporary period of indefinite length the number of immigrants into the United States. We could do this by simply advising our consuls to put every obstacle in the way and to require additional evidence and to resort to various administrative devices which would postpone and postpone and postpone the granting of the visas." Words like *additional evidence*, *temporary* and especially *indefinite* are the types of superficial terms that politicians love to use to give their friends (and themselves) the ability to act with their own discretion.

Frances Perkins, for her part, was still trying to convince her fellow cabinet members to be as liberal as possible with visa and passport laws, expanding immigration quotas past levels that most were comfortable with. Her efforts seemed to be working: a record twenty-seven-thousand-plus Germans entered the country in 1939.

Then, in the summer of 1940, Roosevelt's advisors, including Long, started convincing the president that enemies from abroad could be sneaking in to destroy and steal from the government, a mantra that would form the backbone of much of Long's career. Roosevelt transferred the Immigration and Naturalization Service into the Department of Justice, taking away quite a bit of Perkins's authority.

In 1940, immigration numbers almost matched those of the year before, this time with over 301,000 Germans on the waiting list, but things would fall quickly apart. As World War II loomed closer in the summer of 1941, rules on German immigration were tightened. German Jews looking to come to America could obtain visas only in countries that weren't under Nazi control. The number of those who made it to the United States dropped below 17,000 that year, and the entire waiting list was cancelled. Almost no one could get out—and they wouldn't, at least not to America, as Old Glory joined World War II.

Long had been a major reason why only a few of the *Quanza* passengers managed to debark in New York. When Mexico turned them away, he breathed a sigh of relief, knowing that people were going his way and that the potential enemies on the ship wouldn't be getting in. He'd had help staving off Perkins's challenges. But then another female enemy stepped up to face Long, and Eleanor Roosevelt had quite a bit more weaponry at the ready. Maybe Long could say no to her, at least in a polite way, but her

President Roosevelt's Assistant Secretary of State Breckinridge Long's anti-immigration efforts nearly doomed the SS *Quanza* passengers. *Library of Congress.*

husband could override Long in a quarter of a second. As many around Roosevelt rallied around his wife—and, through her, the *Quanza* folk—Roosevelt decided to act.

He'd prepared for this, sort of. Two years before, the president had established the President's Advisory Committee on Political Refugees to assist thousands, mainly the rich/or prominent in their native lands, in finding safe transport elsewhere. James McDonald was made chair of the High Commission for Refugees (Jewish and Others) Coming from Germany in 1933 and spent two years fighting for Jewish refugees before quitting when he was forced to realize he was fighting alone. Now, as committee chair, he'd get another shot.

McDonald, along with Assistant U.S. Attorney Henry Hart, Solicitor General Francis Biddle and Edward Prichard, who'd been assisting Attorney General Robert Jackson, were ordered to discuss the legal status of the *Quanza* passengers. Very quickly, the group decided that the passengers had a right to apply for visas.

It may or may not have been a personal matter, but Roosevelt contacted Long and explained to him exactly what Long would (not could, should, might or anything else that involved a choice) be doing next in the matter. His assistant secretary would be evaluating the status of the *Quanza* group, along with McDonald and Marshall Field III, who'd worked under Eleanor on the U.S. Committee for the Care of European Children. Long would do what he could to ensure that, even if not all of them got in, the refugees wouldn't get the ice-cold shoulder that Mexico—and, previously, America—had given them. Long would help in any way he could to show that his country was a gracious host. Roosevelt wasn't asking. Long didn't have a choice. He wouldn't forget it.

CHAPTER 10

LONG VS. PERKINS

Now that we've met the Morewitzes, who would wind up as heroes of this piece, let's touch on the lead villain. It's not President Roosevelt, although he'd hardly come off as a prince, at least at first. No, this guy put tremendous effort into imposing suffering on others. But it won't be all bad. We'll also meet a lady who had more guts than most of her male colleagues combined, as many would continue to find out.

As America slowly grasped the darkness overtaking Germany and, ultimately, much of Europe, long before the war officially began, a political chess match broke out behind the scenes of the Roosevelt administration. Breckinridge Long represented the black side, showing so many of the dark ways politicians can abuse authority and the damage, even death, such actions can cause. On the other side was Frances Perkins, determined to be remembered for much more than her gender.

If Roosevelt had any notable weaknesses in his political life, and he certainly had several, one was that he allowed his personal feelings and friendships to override his political sense—as in giving power and positions to his friends, qualifications secondary. Long would be a major beneficiary of this. After serving as President Wilson's secretary of state, he was shellacked in two Missouri senate races in 1920. Roosevelt had a short career in the U.S. Senate before catching on as Wilson's assistant secretary of the navy in 1913 (ironically, his cousin Theodore had been one of Wilson's staunchest opponents). A bout with polio derailed his political career for much of the 1920s, but a one-point victory over state Attorney General Albert Ottinger for the governorship in 1928 was his first step toward political history. When his old friend and Wilson colleague made his first run for the White House in 1932, Long went all out in support—and Roosevelt didn't forget it, handing him the ambassadorship to Italy the next year.

Meanwhile, while Roosevelt had been taking time off to recover, Perkins was working her way up through the New York government in ways—and at speeds—that, arguably, no woman had before. Battles for the Big Apple's labor force won her the begrudging respect of her male colleagues and the public in the 1920s. Roosevelt's governorship win pushed her to become the state's first industrial commissioner, and she spent the next four years right beside him, fighting for stronger protection for women and children.

Rumors about female membership in the presidential cabinet had been discussed for over a decade. But Roosevelt finally put word to action in 1933, making Perkins the first female secretary of labor. To be fair, Perkins and Roosevelt had been pals for some time, so she also benefited from his individual bias to a degree.

On March 4, 1933, Roosevelt was sworn in for the first time. Just five weeks earlier, Adolf Hitler had been handed control of Germany on a pitch-black platter. And no one, in their deepest nightmares, could have guessed anything that would happen next in Germany and much of Europe for over a decade.

CHAPTER 11

MOVING TOWARD NORFOLK

We were absolutely beside ourselves. We were told that we were just going to take on coal and leave. Younger kids on the ship had no idea that there was a chance America didn't want us, either. Who was to say that we'd even be allowed in?
I felt like we were never getting off that ship.
—Malvina Parnes

As the *Quanza* made it through the last few nautical miles to Norfolk, the end of a 2,100-mile journey, word was starting to spread about the passengers' plight. Even as more and more words and photos about the war took up most of the front pages every day, small briefs and then longer articles started to let readers know the good word. It was rare for a ship arriving in port to get any ink at all, let alone statewide coverage, but this was no ordinary docking. The danger the passengers could face wasn't entirely clear, but people were starting to get some ideas, accurate or otherwise. Something needed to be done, even if no one was quite certain what.

"Unless government officials rescind an order issued in August, the refugees will not be permitted to land," blared papers from Hampton Roads to Richmond and even farther (the tale became an Associated Press gold mine, with word getting across the Old Dominion and other states). "The steamer is only calling at this point to replenish her bunkers and will not enter or clear through customs. She is expected to be in port not more than six hours."

Reading that and that alone, most people would have probably shrugged and flipped to the comics section. It was just another ship full of people whom many felt shouldn't be here to begin with. But again, by this point, the *Quanza*'s tale had made its way up and down the East Coast, the media a glad carrier, and people were starting to figure out that there was more to this than the papers could tell without a libel charge.

As the *Quanza* approached, passengers also started reaching out to someone else who might devote a bit of time to their plight for professional and personal reasons. Sol Bloom, an American Jew himself, had been representing New York in Congress since 1929, and he'd become chairman of the House Foreign Affairs Committee a decade later, helping to secure the Truman Doctrine, the Marshall Plan and other political movements during his time and holding two tenures as committee chair. Always a bit more liberal toward refugees than many of his colleagues, Bloom reached out to Cordell Hull and Breckinridge Long to discuss some ways to rescue the *Quanza* group.

We can guess how receptive Long was, but Hull was starting to backtrack a bit. He'd advised Roosevelt to block the *St. Louis* from landing in America and represented America at the Havana Conference in the summer of 1940. When the *Quanza* matter first came about, Hull's response was just as emphatic and negative as it had been toward the previous ship: We don't want you. After Eleanor got involved, however, Hull started to change his mind a bit. As Bloom, Wise and others started to express the same feelings independently, Hull quickly and quietly began to wonder if maybe his original ideas had been too harsh, too much of a rubber stamp on an issue that might deserve some individual attention.

Literally hours before the ship arrived, Hull received an impromptu visitor. Back in 1933, Dr. Nahum Goldmann had barely missed becoming one of Dachau's first residents, lucky (in a sense) enough to be at his father's funeral in Palestine when the Gestapo raided his hometown. He'd helped Wise established the World Jewish Congress and, later, served as its president. Goldmann implored Hull to loosen the laws and his own views. The *Quanza* people had been forced to flee and turned away twice, including from this very country. Regardless of how Hull felt about them or about immigrants in general, one decision, and maybe no further action on his part, could mean their lives. That's a tough proposition to have to live with.

Hull pointed to the American flag in his office. "I took an oath to protect that flag and obey the laws of my country," he raged at Goldmann, "and you are asking me to break those laws."

Goldmann assured him that he wasn't asking to have the laws broken, per se, just stretched and bent the tiniest bit. Laws are meant to be made short and superficial enough to be interpreted and applied one way or another, depending on the matter at hand. What real damage could allowing in a few dozen people do, especially when the quota laws had been so liberally interpreted in the past?

"You," Hull fired back, his voice as narrow and angry as his eyes, "are the most cynical man I have ever met." Though many would vie for that title as World War II raged across Europe and yanked America in, it might have applied to Goldmann then. But Goldmann had heard worse, and he was ready for this.

"I ask you, Mr. Secretary," he inquired, trying not to sound too condescending, "who is the cynical one? I, who wish to save these innocent people, or you, who are prepared to send them back to their death?" Goldmann had kept much more abreast of the Nazis' deeds than much of America or the rest of the world. He knew very well what had happened to far too many and certainly would happen to the *Quanza* group. Hull didn't concede right then and there, but he finally did toss a little support to the passengers. Few people back then were aware that his wife, Rose Frances Whitney, was an Austrian Jew.

Support was growing, and special voices were getting louder. But while newspapers and even politicians can start and support such a movement, it's those on the inside, the locals, who end up making the difference—the people who can get close enough to those with the authority to make the right changes. A nationwide event can be altered by a few people in a small room in a small town that few were aware of just a few days before.

It would take the help of the court system. It would take lawyers making the right arguments. It would require a few signatures by the hands of convinced judges. Here's where the lawyers got called into action. Here's where the Morewitzes come back into our story.

CHAPTER 12

SWIMMER

Actually, just a moment. What follows happened just before Jacob and Sallie Morewitz really stepped into the game, and it's become one of the more well-known tales of the *Quanza* matter. It also factors into the future of our story.

One passenger felt he had nothing to lose, and rightfully so. Hilmar Wolff, formerly a student back at the University of Zurich in Switzerland, had gotten the most unwelcome news the previous June. He was being ordered back to his native Germany to enlist in Hitler's ranks. Wolff was lucky enough to secure a visa in Lisbon (he had missed the German invasion of Belgium the previous May by, it seemed, mere seconds), but like every other passenger, he could feel his luck slipping away after being turned down in New York and Mexico. He could feel the wave of helplessness washing over the sad crew of the *Quanza*, and he decided that even the cold, dark, unfamiliar waters of the Chesapeake Bay were less ominous.

As the ship waited a few miles from Lambert's Point, ready to go in, grab its coal and leave, Wolff decided he couldn't wait for any more disappointments. If he was sent back to Europe, surviving combat would be the best outcome he could hope for. What he was about to do was worth it. Having fallen in love with one of his fellow passengers, who was lucky enough to debark in New York, was an extra incentive.

At around three o'clock in the morning on September 11, when most of the passengers and much of the crew were out like a light for the night, Wolff dressed in regular business attire and bundled up some belongings. Taking a deep breath, he stepped toward the edge of the *Quanza*'s deck. He could see some lights in the distance, and he tried to convince himself that they were a welcoming omen, a guide to safety and security. It's tough to gauge distance across water, especially in the middle of the night, but Wolff knew he'd have a few miles to cover and nowhere to take a breather if he got tired.

Centuries ago, before the United States itself existed, the English explorer John Smith came ashore there, and settlers built a huge wooden structure for soldiers and cannons, labeling it Fort Algernourne (or Algernon, depending on who is writing). During the War of 1812, however, British forces rolled right up to and through the fort, all the way up to Washington, which they captured for a few days in August 1814 before America battled back and won the next January.

President James Madison, convinced that changes needed to be made if Hampton Roads was to maintain its heavy military presence, ordered the fort replaced with a new, much stronger one. Slave laborers, equipped mainly with offerings from rock quarries in Virginia and Maryland, got to work (military convicts would soon take over). In all, workers spent about fifteen years putting together America's largest stone fort, a distinction it still carries. Monroe would branch out over sixty-three acres, nearly a mile and a half in diameter.

But Wolff was holding out hope that another part of the peninsula would live up to its moniker. When Smith and his colleagues first landed, the tired men thanked the area's most southern tip for the "great comfort" it provided on their journey. The area would eventually become known as Point Comfort, and Wolff could only hope it would be as hospitable to him as it was to Smith.

Placing a hand on the guardrail, Wolff maneuvered over it and teetered on the edge of the deck, nothing left between him and the water. He fell. Unsure of the depth of the water, Wolff had decided not to dive, instead landing on his back and legs. The cold and wet already rushing in, he started off. It would be one of the longest journeys of his life, at least in the figurative sense, but if he could make it to freedom, away from the evils he'd heard about and many of his friends had already been pulled into, it would be more than worth it. If he didn't make it, Wolff knew, "his life would be forfeit."

Wolff started to paddle. He was in pretty good shape, at least good enough for the Nazis to want him to fight for them, but this was new: no warning, no warming up, swimming gear that was far short of athletic. But as far as he could know, it was this or death.

The current knocked him back and forth. Jellyfish started using him for target practice. He ingested and regurgitated enough salt water to cover the *Quanza*. Mile after mile, hour after hour, Wolff paddled through the darkness. Septembers in Hampton Roads aren't necessarily freezing, but in the fall, any water gets cold at night, and Wolff could feel his strength slipping away. He liked water well enough, but this was the most impromptu of sea races, all too far from a pool. He lost his shoes, his coat, his pants. He barely had enough feeling in his arms and hands to hang onto his makeshift luggage.

Then his mind suddenly cleared, and his body suddenly felt so much better. He could see the Point, and it didn't seem too far away anymore. Maybe the lights were a sign, welcoming him. He was actually going to make it, he thought. He'd lie on the shore to rest up a bit and then sneak into Hampton. He'd score a new visa, legitimately or otherwise, fictionalize his name and his past and go off to live a whole new, safer life in America.

Not exactly.

As the sun rose over Fort Monroe, guards noticed something in the distance. Perhaps it was a large turtle or some other landlubber animal that had gotten caught in an undertow, maybe even a shark out for a nighttime feeding—uncommon in Hampton Roads but not unheard of. Hell, maybe the Loch Ness monster had a long-lost relative on the other side of the globe. With not much else going on at that time of the morning, they just stood and watched. Whatever it was, it was moving slowly. But if it was a human, it might be armed. He or she, probably the former, might just be a secret agent from another country, armed with a hidden weapon that was just begging to be drawn and fired.

Closer and closer the creature ventured. Slowly, the guards could make out a pair of arms, then a head, then a torso. Okay, so it was human, and it didn't look particularly threatening. Now the mystery was why anyone would be out for a swim at this time of day, at this location—after all, there are several beaches right nearby. Just the month before, the 1940 Olympics had been cancelled over the war, but maybe this fellow was getting started training for the 1944 Games. Sadly, they'd be postponed as well, but no one knew that just yet.

The guards watched as the man moved closer and closer. The package in his hand showed them that he wasn't just out to exercise. Honestly, they couldn't help but feel a bit impressed. It had taken him some time and effort to come this far. But they had a job to do.

As Wolff approached Comfort, his head and shoulders sank, though not enough to drag him underwater. The guards had seen him splashing, he knew. He wasn't going to get away. Maybe he'd be taken prisoner. Maybe the whole ship would be detained and then sent back right away. Maybe these guys would think he was some sort of spy and shoot him right there on sight.

They didn't. The guards just waded out into Mill Creek, the small lake in front of the fort, and pulled Wolff, who had just suffered a serious hand injury during his swim, out of the water—but not too roughly. "It was a case in which we would have been happy to give assistance," a wowed guard marveled, "but we were powerless." Wolff was turned over to immigration authorities.

Just after the Civil War, a fellow named Jefferson Davis spent six months in a cell at this very fort, accused of treason, mistreating Union soldiers and trying to have President Lincoln killed. Power-hungry guards felt their egos swell from being able to treat the former president of the Confederacy as just another crook, sometimes chaining him up in leg irons and guarding him with ominous weaponry. A terrified Wolff feared that he might suffer even worse punishment. But here, he actually got lucky. The lawmen, perhaps as enamored with his plight as the guards had been, took him to a stateroom near the ship and handed him breakfast, "better than the food served to the first-class passengers." Shortly after, a frightened, downcast Wolff was returned to the ship, certain he'd never set foot in America again.

Later that morning, the *Quanza* pulled in to the docks at the Virginia Railway coal pier at Sewell's Point. As far as the passengers had reason to believe, they'd be there only long enough to pick up some fuel and then head straight back to Europe and, most likely, death. But as the ferry from Newport News arrived, some riders hopped right off and went to work to change the hopes and minds of many of their fellow passengers—and possibly a few others.

CHAPTER 13

MORE ABOUT THE MOREWITZES

The other lawyers feared Jacob when they went against him, because he was far into the law. He thought the law came down from Mount Sinai, and he would do everything for his client. He took the cases personally. If the other side badmouthed his client, he would jump right up and object. He thought his clients were all angels, even when they weren't.

—Stephen Morewitz

Like most who had seen war up close and gorily personal, Jacob Morewitz didn't want anyone else to be forced to face it. Those who celebrate war and support those who fight it have rarely seen it themselves. Doing so might severely change their outlook.

Jacob had gotten off to a rough start in school. Grades-wise, he'd been fine, but other issues had arisen. He'd long had an interest in motorcycle racing, but that wasn't something that youths were supposed to do way back before World War I. He was called into the principal's office for a stern lecture on how such a thing wasn't going to be allowed at *this* school. Do *not* bring a motorized two-wheeler into *our* parking lots.

Sorry. This guy was a rebel without (much of) a cause before James Dean was born. The very next day, he drove his trusty transport right up the steps of the school—depending on the source, he may have even taken it into the hallways. He was expelled immediately. None too downtrodden, Jacob (who would keep racing and win titles along the way) roared out of Norfolk's Maury High School and ventured north to the T.C. Williams School of Law at Richmond College, not long before it became the University of Richmond. He then found a place in the maritime law community.

This area of practice isn't one of the most common nationwide, but it's very prevalent in areas with a heavy military presence, particularly a sea-based one, and Hampton Roads has held such a presence since wars started being fought in America. Maritime lawyers have fought both against and in favor of those accused of piracy; made and modified laws on licensing and registration for ships; debated insurance claims; been involved in civil matters between shipowners, crew members, passengers and everyone else; and discussed carriage of goods and passengers, like the case John Quincy Adams fought before the Supreme Court on behalf of the *Amistad* passengers in 1840, one of the biggest early blows against slavery in the United States. Both Alexander Hamilton, who helped ratify the Constitution, and John Adams, who signed the Declaration of Independence and became America's first vice president and second president, worked in maritime law. Judge Oliver Wendell Holmes, before whom Morewitz argued at the Supreme Court, practiced in the area as well.

Morewitz had been the general counsel at Maritime Administration in Washington, D.C., and worked briefly as a legal assistant to the director of the Bureau of Marine Inspection and Navigation in the U.S. Department of Commerce. And Sallie had been there as well. After teaching in the Newport News school system while her husband was at war, she'd made a career switch that few American ladies had ever even considered. In December 1930, she was the first woman from William & Mary to be admitted to the bar. (In 1966, she and Jacob would donate over six hundred books from their personal collection to Sallie's alma mater.)

Ironically, when Sallie was admitted to the bar of the U.S. Court of Appeals for the Fourth Circuit in April 1949, the clerk issued Sallie's degree under the moniker "Sallie Rome Morewitz, Esquiress." But that would come later. Over a decade before the *Quanza* matter, the pair established Morewitz & Morewitz in Newport News and became a new extreme rarity: one of the area's first husband-and-wife legal teams. Sallie knocked out the researched briefs and motions, and her husband physically stood before a judge and argued them. If the pair had been in the movies that helped bail out the American economy during the Great Depression, she'd have been the producer, screenwriter and director, while he'd have been the actor.

Even so, few would know. As judges, opposing lawyers and whoever else looked over the briefs Jacob proudly presented to them, they marveled at the skill of "S.R." or, sometimes, "S. Rome," the moniker in the short bylines. All too aware of how quickly her words would get tossed aside if people knew a lady had sat at the typewriter, Sallie concealed her first name and let her work, literally, speak for itself.

She was just the next in a long list of women forced to hide their own independence. In a trend that continues in fiction today, *Pride and Prejudice* and *Emma* emerged without an author's name on the cover. Even sadder, Jane Austen passed at age forty-one in 1817, never knowing that her books would still be read, discussed and taught over two centuries later. Louisa May Alcott, Charlotte Brontë and many others wrote under male names to avoid the gender issue.

Readers of *The Outsiders*, which has been required reading for generations of English classes and sold enough copies to fill the *Quanza* a few times over, may be aware that it's one of several tomes by S.E. Hinton. However, even today, many are still surprised to learn that those initials stand not for Scott or Steve or Sebastian but for Susan Eloise. When the Oklahoma teenager knocked out the book in 1965, publishers were sure that, years away from the feminist movement of the 1970s, the mostly male reviewer community, along with readers, would toss it aside if her name appeared on the cover.

And yes, this still happens. Since 2013, readers have experienced the adventures of title character private eye Cormoran Strike and his partner Robin Ellacott, all from the pen of Robert Galbraith. With over 20 million Strike novels sold, Galbraith has done pretty well. Problem is, he doesn't exist. For all his success, Strike is only the second-most famous leading male that J.K. Rowling has created—yes, the same J.K. Rowling whose agent convinced her not to go by her full name, sure that readers wouldn't want to read about a young wizard and his friends if they knew a lady had written them. It's just one more example of how so many creations have been ridiculed and disregarded simply because they came from the mind of someone lacking an Adam's apple.

Perhaps in an attempt to camouflage his faith, if not his gender, Jacob often went by his initials rather than his full first name, as decades of newspaper articles show.

As Ralph Josephson told them the *Quanza* tale, the Morewitzes recalled that, on a smaller scale, they'd been here before. Almost exactly sixteen years previously, in September 1924, Jacob Morewitz stood in a Newport News courtroom and filed a habeas corpus writ on behalf of four crew members of the steamer *Roxen*. The men claimed they'd been held captive above the Swedish ship, and Morewitz fought to get them off, physically and legally. It worked: Just before the ship was to head back to its homeland, a judge agreed and ordered their release. But the very next day, Morewitz added to the movement: He filed a lawsuit alleging libel against the *Roxen* crew.

The term *libel* is commonly associated with unfairly defaming someone in print. In maritime law, however, it has a different meaning. Morewitz was claiming that his clients' liberties had been cruelly stolen. The ship and its company had mistreated the men too many times and broken their contract with them, and now Morewitz was going to make them pay, or at least try. The crew members had been treated the same as prisoners thrown in jail for a crime someone else had committed, and they deserved compensation.

Morewitz had some help. Shortly before this, the Treasury Department had ordered that foreign seamen be kept aboard their ships while they were in American ports, and the Chamber of Commerce Foreign Trade Bureau and Hampton Roads Maritime Exchange had fought this. The Seamen's Act of 1915 gave seamen the right to sue for half their wages. Morewitz used their arguments in his own suit and asked for over $5,000 in damages.

The following January, the suit was overturned and dismissed, as a judge ruled that an American court—at least this one—had no jurisdiction to hear the case, let alone award damages. That was fine; the men were free and clear from their impromptu imprisonment. The *Roxen* doctrine, still around today, clarified that the 1915 Seamen's Act indeed applied to foreigners in U.S. waters, and it's been used in cases extending to sailors' race, religion, gender and everything else that has led to discrimination.

In November 1929, a month after the stock market crash plunged America toward the Great Depression, Morewitz roared all the way to the Supreme Court on behalf of the estate of *Hybert* sailor C.A. Barford, who'd been killed on the job in Norfolk the year before. The sailor died when a ship's lifeboat fell on him on the dock, a court later ruling that the lifeboat was out of repair. It wouldn't be the last time the Morewitzes would be seen in America's highest court. But again, that's for a later chapter.

The Morewitzes were in demand. Their skills and successes had become well known, and their client list kept getting longer. And yes, they were also working with both a huge asset and a growing liability: their faith. It wasn't a popular time to be an American Jew, especially with anti-Semitism slowly rising across America as the Nazi regime strengthened overseas. As recently as the 1920s, the University of Virginia had instated official quotas to limit the number of Jewish students admitted, and many other schools had already done the same—a number that would also rise.

Sallie and Jacob Morewitz, one of the only husband-wife legal teams in 1940 Hampton Roads, ended up as the driving force behind the rescue of dozens from the Holocaust. *Courtesy of* Pauline Leger/*Nobody Wants Us* film.

Just weeks before the *Quanza* matter came around, Jacob represented five Jewish sailors who'd staged a sit-in against the masters of the Finnish steamer *Edit H.*, refusing to return to their ship, which had made it to Norfolk from France, due to alleged mistreatment. The men were held in Norfolk for over a month before he won their release.

Josephson hoped that the Morewitzes, who had helped create Newport News's Rodef Sholem Synagogue in 1921, would find it in themselves to help those facing the exact same bigotry they themselves had faced, or at least heard of. The Morewitzes had long been popular with Hampton Roads' Jewish population, which had reached into the twenty thousands, and now they could make a difference that might just reach across America.

"They were very busy, suing ships up and down the cases," says Stephen Morewitz, Jacob and Sallie's grandson. "My grandfather was a great champion of the underdog. The family motto with my grandparents was, 'Ready for trial, your honor.'"

With Sallie knocking out the briefs and Jacob ready to argue them, it was time to put that motto to work yet again. No reason to fix what's already working fine. With the ship getting closer every day, the Morewitzes tossed themselves straight into fighting for the Rands and maybe some more. They knew other lawyers would be involved, and they just hoped no one would get greedy. Dozens of passengers were there, but they all wanted the same thing: just one small gift of freedom. Sallie and Jacob were confident that if they could convince the right people, or even just one person, that their clients had the right to walk across to the mainland, others would follow suit.

Once again, this was a fight they'd won before. It was time to do it again now and hope it worked—not for the money, not for the prestige, just for those on the *Quanza* who needed someone to finally be able to believe in.

CHAPTER 14

MOREWITZ ARRIVES

As the ferryboat made its way across the Chesapeake Bay that September morning, Jacob Morewitz stood near the side rail, hoping to get a glimpse of his immediate future. Perusing that day's edition of the *Daily Press* had already given the young lawyer plenty to worry about. The day before and that very morning, the Nazi army had handed Britain its largest attack in the English land's history, dropping enough bombs all over London to injure thousands, kill hundreds and devastate the world's proudest lands. If no one could stop the German military—and Britain admitted it had been nowhere near ready that day—there might be little Americans could do to prevent the war from reaching their shores. With its heavy military presence, Hampton Roads might be one of the first targets.

Morewitz stood and stared. Through the light September rain, he thought he could make it out. He hoped.

An outsider wouldn't have noticed anything out of place that day; even a new ship might not stand too far out in a place like Sewell's Point, where ships pulled in and out every morning, noon and night. Morewitz, though, had something special to look for. His eyes made their way across ship after ship. Some docks at the Point had a few; others were almost bare. Some were clearly created for military combat, so he could quickly eliminate them. But there were a few that just might be his next destination, where his clients and their fellow passengers had gone from relieved passengers on their way to freedom to something just one step from captivity. Was that the *Quanza*? Or could it be this one? Maybe the one next to that? He'd find it soon enough.

The ferryboat pulled up in Norfolk. Morewitz watched his fellow passengers find their cars and go. He held back. It would give him a little extra time to think. He'd end up having a bit more time than he anticipated: the ship wouldn't actually be there until about ten o'clock that morning. As Morewitz stepped onto the dock to wait, he recognized several legal colleagues from around the area.

Ralph Josephson had told the sad, scary tale of his friend Moritz Rand and the rest of the Rand family. Like so many others, the Rand family's hopes had been dashed time and again, and this might be the last chance they would see. Morewitz had said yes. But now he had a different plan. This wasn't going to be "just" a contract-breaking battle. He was starting to truly grasp the plight that his clients and the rest of the ship faced.

As the ship finally pulled in, Morewitz saw more and more *Quanza* folk coming to the deck, looking over the Norfolk seaboard. But in contrast to the optimism the group had felt and shown in the first two stops, these were looks of despair and hopelessness. Passengers were milling around, filling themselves with wishful thinking, gazing at a land that had denied them twice and would be cruel enough to do so again.

Morewitz and the rest of his legal colleagues glanced over the sad, tired but still desperately optimistic eyes and faces of their new clientele. And if the *Quanza* group had the smallest of reasons to believe, it was that at least some of their efforts had rung true—not just for the lawyers that people like Josephson had helped them contact but for others who had heard of them and shown up as well.

Cecila Razovsky and Elise Margolius of the National Council of Jewish Women were there—both far more in tune than the general public with the genocide that was already going far too strong in Germany (Auschwitz, considered the world's most infamous concentration camp, had been established the previous May, and several others existed as well). Razovsky, who was also high up in the National Refugee Service, had hinted that representatives from the U.S. State Department could show up. Several other prominent Hampton Roads Jews were also on the dock that day. The American Committee for Christian-German Refugees had sent representative Evelyn Hersey to further its mission of removing those who were in danger from Germany. Of course, members of the local press were out in droves. It was a pretty good start, and others might be arriving soon.

And, of course, there were local friends and family of the *Quanza* group. Morewitz could feel their pleading eyes on him as well. Could he be their savior?

Well, planting a staff and parting the Chesapeake Bay, giving his people a way to jump off the boat and walk over, probably wouldn't be effective; cops would just wait on the other side and arrest everyone, just as they had Wolff. And Morewitz certainly didn't have the four decades that Moses got to lead the Israelites through the desert; he didn't even have forty hours to work with.

Lesser attorneys might have seen it as a problem. He considered it just an obstacle, which every case has in some form. He'd taken on this burden when he said okay to Josephson, and now it was his to carry, even if it was one of the heavier loads of his life. He knew where to begin. He knew where he hoped to finish. Now it was a matter of connecting the two.

CHAPTER 15

MOREWITZ TAKES ACTION

Here's where we really get into the gist of the story, especially as it pertains to the role that the Morewitz family and the city of Norfolk—along with much of Hampton Roads, the state of Virginia and places even farther away—played in it. To make it easier to follow, we're literally going to take this one day at a time. It's amazing how many changes can take place over a few days.

September 11, Morning

Morewitz on the Quanza

Had a fresh shipment of coal already been available at Sewell's Point that morning, it could have meant death for the passengers.

When Captain Herberts had docked at Norfolk, he wasn't even considering the issue of disembarking. It had hardly been raised. He hadn't expected to have to worry about this.

As the ship was scheduled to take just a few hours to fill up, the local customs community hadn't even been notified. Any official with much thoroughness to the job might have come onboard and learned just how amiss things truly were on the *Quanza*, but ships that were planning to spend less than a day in port without sending anyone to shore weren't required to check in. If coal had been there right then, the *Quanza* would have been out of port by that evening.

But perhaps fate was smiling on the passengers for the first time in weeks; there wasn't enough fuel available for a fill-up, so the ship would be around for some time. In a profession known for slow motion, Morewitz and his legal colleagues went on fast-forward. If they didn't convince certain people to make the slightest move that very day, they might not get another shot, and neither would their clientele. The lawyers would have a job to do and a new person to fight for, and with, the very next day. Those on the ship might not live to see the next month.

As the ship waited near a grain elevator at the Virginia Railway's coal pier, Captain Herberts ordered it loaded down with armed guards, fearing that more passengers would attempt to follow Wolff's escape route, so much so that the guards nearly prevented Morewitz from climbing aboard to finally meet the clients that Josephson had informed him of. But when he was finally on the ship, with some of Sallie's briefs to guide him, Morewitz discussed his new plan with the Rands.

By this point, many *Quanza* passengers had reached out to the local legal community, and most of the hired help had gone the quick way. One after another had looked back into the bounds of the law and found the words *habeas corpus*. At the outset, it might have looked like a safe bet. Speaking broadly, the procedure allows a lawyer to claim that their clients have been unlawfully detained or imprisoned and seek a court appearance so that a judge can make the final decision. Looking over the ice-cold shoulder the *Quanza* passengers had been given both in New York and Mexico, it would be tough to argue that they'd received any kind of fair treatment.

But there were some potential problems with that strategy, as the lawyers and their clients were already starting to discover. First off, all a judge had to do was disagree. Such laws are vague and wide because they have to be. That's why opposing lawyers can argue over what laws mean, beyond what they say. Interpretation is a major key to the American legal system, and rights violations are a huge component therein. It's all too commonplace to hear, "My client's rights were violated under *this* law, *that* statute, *this* amendment, and here's why!" and then get the response, "Oh no they weren't, and *here's* why!"

A judge simply had to pull out a different viewpoint. If a lawyer was unlucky enough to find himself in front of a judge with an opposing, personal or otherwise, definition of words like *unlawful*, *unequal* and/or *unfair*, the case was over right then and there. A judge could check over and dismiss the motion in less time than it would take to read this page. And even if the jurist was feeling a little charitable, all that could be done was to hold a

The lives of dozens of passengers aboard the SS *Quanza* finally changed for the good on September 14, 1940, as they were permitted to deboard at Sewell's Point in Norfolk. *Courtesy of Norfolk Public Library.*

hearing with the client present. The judge would be able to just listen, rule and move on, and there was little reason to believe that anyone else would make a different decision.

And the clients already had another strike against them. They were outsiders, new to this land, and many in and out of the justice system didn't hold such folk in high regard—at least, not high enough to consider them entitled to the same rights as those born here in America. According to the law, judges are required to leave their personal beliefs back in chambers. But this is human nature we're talking about, and even those who swear by the law might just leave it behind sometimes. Too many judges felt, secretly, that foreigners just didn't deserve what Americans had worked so hard for.

However, a few had been lucky enough to find at least some reprieve. Mere hours (if that) after meeting their clients, the legal community deluged the local courts with enough briefs and motions to sink the *Quanza* itself. If a shipment of coal just happened to arrive early, the crew would load it up and get going, and the law enforcement community wouldn't have grounds to act; the court order that had kept the *Quanza* passengers onboard in New York was still in effect. If the ship pulled out, the lawyers knew, it was unlikely a judge would find it worth the time and trouble to call it back.

The lawyers had to act right then and there. Out of so many attempts, a few had to get through, and they did. But as Morewitz explained to the Rands, and those eavesdropping nearby, he had a different plan. This one didn't really involve winning; he didn't necessarily need a judge to agree with him for it to work, not right away. Rather than go the fast way, he decided to attack the legal system in a way that would get its attention.

Money. Morewitz was out for it, and a lot of it—not really for him or even for his clients, but more against the people who put his clients in this situation. He'd have certainly loved to go straight at the people who cruelly left his people on the ship just a few states north and then a country south, but that wasn't possible, not just yet. Morewitz was going straight after the shipping company. He was going to make them pay, quite literally, for putting everyone in this situation.

Shove a six-figure lawsuit in someone's face, and they're going to listen. This wasn't the kind of suit that a judge could just slam down a gavel and dismiss. He'd be in a ton of people's faces about this, not just one judge in one courtroom: several different arguments, several different targets. But as nice as gobs of green can be, they weren't his end goal. Morewitz doubted he'd see much personally, nor would his clients. That was clear from the moment he took the case.

There was something else more important at stake here, and that was time: time for the word to spread, hopefully past the borders of Hampton Roads, and time for more people to get involved. Morewitz had heard rumblings of the passengers reaching pretty high for help, and there was the chance that someone might just say yes, someone with far more weight than him. Morewitz wanted to bring more and more into the fold. Some, he would be all but forcing to act. He hoped and prayed that others would as well.

"If he doesn't help us get off the ship," Rand admitted, "I don't know what will become of us."

Back at their office, Sallie had been up around the clock, typing out one brief after another to lead her husband through their new plight. "I have to quickly prepare this paperwork," Sallie remembered thinking, "so that Jacob can bring it all to both the U.S. District Court and the coast guard in Norfolk. They're going to sail away if he doesn't get over there to put this claim in immediately."

With her voluminous map in his briefcase, Morewitz raced around downtown Norfolk. There were people to see, briefs to drop off, arguments to make and people to save from humanity's worst.

September 11, Afternoon

Morewitz in Court

As afternoons in federal court went, this one had been regularly routine: bonds being issued or denied; motions getting signed; cases getting scheduled, continued, whatever else. There was hardly a moment to breathe, but it was nothing the Norfolk federal district court clerk's office couldn't handle or hadn't seen before. And then, right around three o'clock in the afternoon, all hell broke loose.

Now we meet the next major player in the case: Judge Luther Way, who, perhaps not intentionally, held the fate of dozens in his gavel-banging hands.

An attorney roared into court, a brief and motion in hand. Then another. Then some more. There were enough petitions to fill Judge Way's courtroom and enough attorneys to load up the nearby Myers Field ballpark, where Yogi Berra, Whitey Ford and so many others would play minor league ball before moving up to the New York Yankees. The lawyers were all there for about the same reason, though some took different approaches. Local law school man Henry Bowden led the charge, armed with a trust habeas corpus writ. He'd been hired by *Quanza* passenger Vladimir Zimmerman, and now it was time to convince Judge Way that certain people were holding Zimmerman on the ship as if it was a city jail. Following him were Sidney Kelsey and James Barron, who were making the same complaint on behalf of others aboard. So many showed up that the office stayed open for nearly an extra hour that night.

Faced with the sudden onslaught, Judge Way snapped right into control. After a few years in the U.S. Department of Justice, he'd been gifted a spot on the U.S. District Court for Virginia's Eastern District by President Herbert Hoover almost a decade before, and these were *his* courts. Like many jurists of the time, he'd borne witness to a bankruptcy barrage during the Great Depression and several booze-related legal wars before Prohibition went away, so this might have been a welcome change. Way wasn't too well informed on the *Quanza* matter, and he certainly wasn't ready for the courtroom siege, but he went into writ action fast.

The first news wasn't good for the visitors. The judge rescinded all the pleas. He didn't think that they were actionable, not like this and not just yet. Again, this was one of those cases where a judge's individual, if not entirely personal, viewpoints can come into play in court. Judges like to get things done and out of the way and move on to the next matter, not sit around and preside over lengthy trials.

Still, if Way had stopped there, or if someone else hadn't roared up to him, the matter might have been put to rest with a few signatures. But Way took another fortunate step that may have saved everything. He ordered Captain Herberts to show up in his court to discuss the matter—the next morning. Again, if Herberts had been allowed to appear that evening and made the right arguments, the ship could have loaded up on fuel and departed. This bought the passengers some time.

"After considering the matter," Way said, "not only for the petitioners and master, but for the public interest of the United States, it is the view of the court that all parties, including the United States, should be given a chance to be heard." Ironically, Way had nearly handled Morewitz's recent case against the *Edit H.* but had taken a last-minute vacation and handed it off to another judge.

Then came Morewitz. He and Sallie had formed a different plan. Morewitz decided to go for an area that couldn't be brushed aside. He went straight for where he could seriously hurt those in charge. He knew just how to get their attention and keep it: by talking not just a few nickels and dimes but big dough.

Morewitz walked straight into court and spoke the magic L-word that's been a boon in civil cases for generations, the same one he'd used over a decade before for his *Roxen* clients and the same one he'd already used in fourteen other such cases: libel. The attorney slapped a $100,000 suit into Way's docket. Six figures is quite a bit even now—in 1940, it was the equivalent of over $2.2 million today. Yes, someone was going to take this a little more seriously.

Morewitz had decided to go at the *Quanza*'s owners back in Portugal. He was claiming that they had wrongfully charged the passengers for delivery, knowing full well that the group wouldn't be able to disembark. After all, everyone, including said owners, recalled the *St. Louis* issue. Morewitz was absolutely certain and willing to shout from the rooftops that his clients were naïve, hardworking innocent folk who'd been duped by a company that should have known this was going to happen, just as it had before. Who cared if he could prove it? The question was this: Could such an argument result in enough stalling to bring in more people with the mindset of Wise, Roosevelt, Bloom and so many others?

Soon after, another welcome inconvenience—for Morewitz and those with him—arose. Leon Seawall, the attorney representing the *Quanza*'s owners, Portuguese National Line, claimed that a bond to battle the libel charge couldn't be raised right away. Decades before e-mail and even the fax machine, cable correspondence with Portugal wasn't at his fingertips. The owners wanted their ship back as soon as possible; without it to transport goods, let alone people, they were losing money.

Seawall, who'd battled Morewitz in court in the past, made a few claims for the ship and against the refugees. First, he argued that the habeas corpus writs were invalid because of an executive order Roosevelt had signed the previous June 5 that required new, tighter documentation for refugees. He also brought forth that since Hampton Roads was not an official military port, inspections should not take place.

Way didn't buy it. He told Seawall to get in touch with the ship's people and get them ready to talk. For Morewitz, it was showtime. He first decided to take testimony from ship's officers and onboard travel agents about harassment of the Rand family. Ship workers testified that the captain had ordered a doctor to confiscate the Rands' passports but hadn't bothered anyone else. Just after Morewitz left the ship for court, an agent pressured the Rands to sign legal documents saying they had not authorized him to file suit. One agent testified that a passenger had "said the Rand family was signing something, and he was going to get them because they had spoiled everything for everybody."

September 12

More and More Get Involved

We were teary, frightened, and sure that we weren't ever
going to be able to get off the ship in America. I was peering out,
crying and nervously twitching.
—Malvina Parnes

Over the next few days, Jacob Morewitz wished he could turn himself into twins or sextuplets. Every morning, he was up before the sun to take the ferry across the bay. Long into the night, he somehow staggered back.

All day, he ventured all over Norfolk, barging into one legal building after another, dropping argument after argument on the desks of those who needed convincing and then voicing the words on the page until his vocal cords were on the verge of rebellion.

He vowed to depose everyone involved with the matter, short of Eleanor Roosevelt herself—and maybe her, if she was available. He was going to have in-depth discussions with the passengers, whether he represented each individual or not; the crew; the ship company's representatives; everyone down to the pier's custodial staff. After all, there was no telling what they might have seen. Morewitz even filed complaints with the U.S. Coast Guard, hoping to show that the ship had been unseaworthy from the start. How dare the *Quanza* company put this twin-screwed piece of rubble out on the water for a single person, let alone hundreds?

He was talking to anyone who would listen, whether he had to force them to do so or otherwise. Lawyers are quite dangerous when they have nothing to lose, and that was certainly the case here. The more debates he could start, the more people he could get involved, voluntarily or involuntarily, the harder it would be to brush him aside like the habeas corpus writs that others had filed. His experience with the *Roxen* matter had shown him that, in this case, winning certainly wouldn't happen anytime soon, and it wasn't really necessary. What mattered was time: getting as much of it as he could and hoping that the group behind him would grow beyond the passengers and the local aid community. His original $100,000 asking price was supplemented to $140,000. And now actual damages were in the game: punitive damages, that is. Morewitz was charging that the plaintiffs had "put the [passengers] in such abject fear as to leave them in an impaired mental and physical state."

Eventually, those making the decisions might just give up from being tired of his relentlessness. That was fine with him. If the right judges or rule makers were to throw up their hands and say, "Hell with it! We've got other cases to try! Let these people stay just to shut that Morewitz guy up!"—that was fine with him.

State Department officials worked all day and night to determine the status of the *Quanza* individuals, holding conferences all over Washington and Northern Virginia. Right in the middle of a hearing in Judge Way's courtroom, an announcement came that the State Department was stepping in, and Way immediately postponed everything going on with the case. No one would be permitted to do much more than take a deep breath until other people straightened this out.

A family shared what precious moments they could as SS *Quanza* passengers waited for lawyers and judges in Norfolk decide if they could stay. *Courtesy of Norfolk Public Library.*

One official admitted,

> *It is practically trial by jury. Because a person has a passport to enter America or one entitling their holder, on the face of the paper, to pass through America en route to another country, is no reason why that particular person will be admitted to roam at will on our shores. We must know something about the holder of the papers, why he or she finds it necessary to seek entrance into the United States, even on a temporary basis when it is possible to return to the original port of debarkation and obtain new passports if those they have are faulty. There are some refugees aboard the* Quanza, *probably a good many, who are entitled to refuge in this country, pending a final disposition of their status. There may be persons aboard the ship who might be agents for foreign countries, seeking a means to enter America or even Mexico for the purposes of stirring up trouble. Those who we find to be refugees fleeing from the vengeance of Adolf Hitler, and who should be given refuge here, will, in all probability, be permitted to land until they can continue their voyage to countries where they can live in peace.*

Still, even as a deputy marshal climbed onto the ship to gleefully inform Captain Herberts that he'd better get comfortable for the time being, whatever progress Morewitz and others had made was unknown to the passengers—especially when the coal finally arrived. Passengers, their lungs already aggravated by the trip, coughed and hacked their way through the dense dark fog that represented a new shade on their path to freedom. The Koppers Coal Company arrived with enough pitch-black carbon to get the ship back to Europe. Ironically, Koppers had been launched a few decades before by engineer Heinrich Koppers, himself a German immigrant.

"We are going back to Lisbon and, perhaps, to Hitler," one passenger sadly admitted, "where our lives won't be worth anything."

As the sun went down that rainy evening, passengers could feel their hopes darkening with the skies. Well-wishers paraded up and down the decks to offer support. Family members shouted to each other from the pier and the ship. Immigration officers held back family members who were trying to grab and hold each other. Some were able to step close enough to whisper to their loved ones, promising they'd soon be together—a promise they could only hope someone else would help them keep.

"There was a momentary ray of light," wrote a passenger, "and everything turned dark again….I don't want to lose my courage no matter what—I don't want to give up. I'll start again; perhaps we'll succeed in escaping somewhere."

One young mother clutched her children to her. "I thought America was the land of the free," she called desperately to her husband on the docks.

"We'll fix it," he promised. "We just need to get a transit visa. That's all. We'll get it."

"Do whatever you can to get us ashore, even if it is only until the war is over," one woman told a news reporter.

On the deck stood Bela Kakenyessy, a few precious feet from his wife and three-year-old son. "I have done everything possible to have them with me, but a cruel law keeps us apart," he said.

Friends and family passed cakes and candy to children onboard ship; custom officials inspected it. Some friendly folk placed Annette Schamroth on a chair attached to a pulley and then lowered her so her dad could give her a doll. "I remember him reaching a hand up to ours," she said. "My sister wondered why we weren't allowed off. I was so scared I was going to fall into the water." She didn't, but the doll didn't last, as one of her bratty young fellow passengers threw it to its own watery grave.

September 13

Getting Political

The stories started off local and quickly spread nationwide. Newspapers were filled with heart-wrenching human interest tales of family separation and the helplessness of the individual against the government. Radio shows literally told millions about the *Quanza* passengers' plight; television news, still in its infancy, hadn't taken off yet. Ironically, the Pearl Harbor attacks the next year would be one of the driving forces to shove TV news across the country.

Earlier that very day, Nazi forces had bombed London for the fourth time in as many days, dropping one straight on Buckingham Palace and driving the week's death toll past 1,100. Perhaps worried about being seen as the same suppressive Gestapo agents they had vowed to keep out of America, the *Quanza* bosses started allowing more visitors onto the ship. Families weren't permitted just yet; that could trigger a riot. Instead, local organization members and authorities were allowed to bring the passengers food. And the press was allowed onboard as well. Many passengers were all too happy to get their story out into the open.

On one side of the ship was Prince Stanislaus Gielski of Poland, anxiously waiting for his bodyguard, Theodore DeJong. "I want Theo so badly I could cry," he said. "He saved my life twice when we were fighting the Germans. He carried me out of a building that had been bombed just before the walls fell. I would have been crushed to death. He got me to safety when the Germans took Warsaw. It was largely through his efforts that I reached…the United States. I just can't do anything without him." Captain E.R. Maximillian Mantner, formerly of the Czech army, had gotten off the *Quanza* in New York. Now he had driven south to help his countrymen and countrywomen off the ship.

Meanwhile, back in D.C., Breckinridge Long battled his way out of his own public relations onslaught. On September 12, he'd attempted to stem the flood by stating, "The State Department will waive visas for aliens aboard the SS 'Quanza' in the following cases: 1. Children; 2. Aliens holding valid visas for other countries than the United States; 3. Bona fide political refugees whom the President's Advisory Committee on Political Refugees will certify for admission."

The first one's pretty self-explanatory. The next two are iffy. Long was quite aware of his boss's and colleagues' fear of spies and figured that the vagueness of his own statement would allow them to keep denying the refugees admittance. Visas for which "other countries" were acceptable? What constituted a "bona fide" visitor, and who would be willing to take the time to certify them rather than just say, "No, you can't come in. Get back on the ship and get off our continent"?

Long was, he claimed, "flooded with pressure groups and telegrams and telephones and personal visits to permit" the passengers to leave the boat and enter the United States.

Long and Roosevelt had a short discussion on the matter. Long had hoped it would be longer. It appeared, he admitted, that Roosevelt "did not want to talk to me on the subject, and I inferred—and it now seems correctly so—that he would leave the matter entirely in my hands"—wishful thinking by him.

Baltimore District Immigration Commissioner Albert R. Archibald, after hearing several stories (none of which lined up, in the factual sense) about the refugees' troubles in New York and Veracruz, headed up a team of immigration officials and made his way down to Norfolk to get the real story. Claiming that each case would be checked over for individual merit, Archibald vowed to return to Washington, D.C., as soon as possible to make some decisions. Assistant U.S. Attorney Harry Holt was also stepping into the matter.

Soon, a new possibility was raised. Perhaps the passengers could be granted the same rights as some of the incoming foreign seamen the Morewitzes had already fought for. In this case, they'd receive a sixty-day visa to step onto

American soil. It sounded like a great deal to the passengers, but nothing was finalized.

Immigration officials, both open and undercover, went back onboard to examine the passengers once again. Consular agents from Belgium, France and other countries did some passport checks.

As the stories kept finding their way across radio shows and into newspapers (remember that back then, most papers had both a morning and an evening edition, so people could read in print about the happenings of earlier that day), locals continued to step in, in the form of organizations that specialized in this sort of action. If the Morewitzes and the rest of the local legal community had suddenly become a team working to win the release of the *Quanza* captors, the remainder of the Hampton Roads community suddenly expanded and did more than its part to finish the welcoming job.

Ever since the ship landed, the dock had been crowded with friends and family, hoping to hear some good news from the courts. Reporters had come by to take photos and do interviews. Of course, some sightseers and well-wishers were around to get a closer look at the new visitors. But now came a bit more organization in the assistance department. Certain companies had been created for situations just like this very one. Others showed up not on their own but as representatives of these groups.

Back when the ship landed in New York, the Hebrew Immigrant Aid Society had attempted to get all the passengers off. That didn't work to the extent it had hoped, but now a few workers hurried south for a second chance. The American Jewish Joint Distribution Committee had been helping Jews escape from Nazi evil since the party had come to power, and now it had a new chance to do so right here at home.

When Cecilia Razovsky first learned of the *Quanza* matter, she didn't bother delegating. For nearly a decade, she'd been the associate director of the National Council of Jewish Women (founded in 1893, around Razovsky's second birthday, it's the oldest organization of its kind in American history), and she'd represented the council in Vienna in 1932 at the First World Conference of Jewish Women. Razovsky also made her way to Norfolk, but not before contacting Hampton Roads' president of the council.

Along with other council members, Elise Margolius had been teaching classes to help Jewish immigrants integrate into American ways, and she hoped to have a few *Quanza* passengers as her next students. Margolius had just organized an emergency committee with the National Refugee Service to get supplies aboard the *Quanza*, and she jumped at the chance to take some there herself. "While they're stuck here on this ship," vowed Margolius,

President of the Norfolk Council of Jewish Women Elise Margolius was gifted dolls by a *Quanza* passenger. *Courtesy of Karen Plotnick.*

whose grandmother Jamie established the Norfolk chapter of the council in 1905, "the least we can do is try to comfort them with kosher meals. Our plan is to fill our cars with as many people as we can." Forming an impromptu "Port and Dock" community, Margolius and fellow council members dined with passengers for their first few nights.

As Margolius stood on the pier handing off soft-spoken motivational speeches to her impromptu audience, a doll landed right beside her, and then another. Someone, probably one of the dozens of youths onboard, was thanking her in the only way possible at that point. Today, those dolls sit in a shadow box in her granddaughter's Virginia Beach home.

Local hotels filled up with family, friends and visitors of both the personal and professional sort. A legal colleague of the Morewitzes, Chuck Kaufman, had helped a few immigrants escape from Germany in 1933 and personally housed them at his place. He'd gotten a reputation for helping out more incomers from China and other countries. Now he'd be fighting for the *Quanza* group as well, as would Walter Rosenberg and his family, who were there to cheer on the passengers. "When we got the call, we answered," remembered Rosenberg. "The way they were putting people in concentration camps looked like they would be killing them. Of course, in those days, I did not know the complete story, just that they were escaping death."

As one more day of uncertainty wound down, former Antwerp resident David Schamroth stood on the dock. Like the Parnes family's father, he'd managed to get to America ahead of the rest of his family. Now, as they must have seemed to Mr. Parnes, the few feet between him and his family seemed as wide as the Pacific itself. "Why can't I have my wife and children with me?" Schamroth shouted. "Should not the law of God rule equally as high as the law of man?"

September 14

Finally, Some Good News

The day before had felt especially bleak for many on and off the ship. It was, after all, Friday the Thirteenth. The next morning didn't have a particularly uplifting start itself. "Immigration authorities," reported a local newspaper headline about the *Quanza* case, "are making careful check of those who seek entry and some, it is reported, may be held as undesirables." Things like this take time. If the headline was accurate, if anything was going to go right for the *Quanza* passengers, it wasn't going to happen anytime soon.

As the day passed, *Quanza* folk tried to keep their spirits up. The groups on the dock kept reassuring them that a winning battle was almost over, and Morewitz was still working hard in the Norfolk court system. He was asking for a hundred grand to get attention. The guards stationed on the nearby boats and on the pier were demonstrating the epitome of wrongful detention. The crew had terrified his clients and the rest of the staff into mental submission. Morewitz had upped his demand an extra $40,000.

Then news started coming in—the best sort. Working with the Marshall Field Committee, which supervised child refugees, and the McDonald Committee, which worked with political refugees, Cordell Hull announced that twenty-five *Quanza* passengers who fit the profile of the two organizations would be getting to land.

And now Patrick Malin steps all the way into our story. A representative of the President's Advisory Committee on Political Refugees, Malin had been battling inequality since becoming a member of the American Civil Liberties Union in the 1920s; a decade after the *Quanza* matter, he'd become the ACLU's executive director. President Roosevelt had assigned Malin to handle *Quanza*. He rushed through report after report on the passengers from both the National Refugee Service and the American Committee for Christian Refugees.

Right in the midst of debating landing card issuance, Malin got a phone call. "[Breckenridge] Long informed me that he was displeased at the number of persons entering under the President's Advisory Committee procedure," Malin later wrote. "I informed him that they were already landing under the supervisor of the immigration inspectors, and he replied simply that he would not himself be responsible for it." Basically, it was the diplomatic, political version of "I matter now, not you." Sadly, such a declaration wouldn't last against Long.

Annette Schamroth, the *Quanza*'s youngest passenger at age three, and her dad celebrate her arrival in Norfolk. *Courtesy of Norfolk Public Library*.

Like Morewitz and so many others, Malin didn't take long to comprehend the weight of the decision before him, the dangers that awaited if he didn't pick a certain way. So he did. Right around nightfall, word of his decision reached the *Quanza* group. "I was astonished, as well as pleased, to note the apparently high quality in terms of personality, intellect, and economic substance of nearly all of the group," Malin asserted. "A decision needs to be made. There's not enough time to contact Europe for more documentation, so I'm recommending that everyone who wants to come ashore, should come ashore."

Just before the sun started to go down, immigration officials boarded with the news. Morewitz and the passengers had only had to convince the right people with the right type of authority to make a few decisions. And they finally had.

Bela Kakenyessy's daughter Christine was one of the first children off the ship. Annette Schamroth was there as well. Both were three years old. Many of those watching clapped and cried. Bursts of cheers and laughter erupted from both the ship and the dock. Several people even hugged and shook hands with the officials.

Ironically, Wolff was one of the first grownups to hit the ground. Maybe the passengers felt that his gutsy aquatic move earlier entitled him to something special. He'd eventually be deemed a legitimate political refugee and escape to Uruguay.

"The very air seems freer," exclaimed passenger Beatrix Boyko, a former skating champion back in her homeland and future physiotherapist in America. Sallie, Jacob and their son Burt, himself a future maritime attorney, celebrated and wept with the Rand family.

More and more passengers trudged off the ship. For some, the excitement and relief they felt at finally making it to safety wasn't quite enough to overcome the mental and physical exhaustion they'd been put through.

While some of the passengers were leaving, others huddled one last time to put together a message to far more people than they could ever thank or even meet. "We hope to remain in this glorious country for a while," read the note, which would eventually make its way into the *Washington Post*, "until we go to our respective new countries. We shall take with us undying memories of true democratic and human kindness, which gave us new courage to start life afresh in a new world."

Lebeau and Dalio staggered off, on their way up to New York. Dalio actually considering kissing Jacob in thanks. "We laugh, we weep, we cannot believe it," Dalio wrote in his memoir. "It seems to be that an enormous Bible has appeared in the heavens, behind which stands God who has just winked at me."

Lebeau was slightly less upbeat. She'd spend the next two months in a hospital in New York and then venture farther north to Montreal. Her last dollars grabbed her a passport back into America and a plane ticket to Hollywood, where fellow French immigrant Charles Boyer helped her get an apartment and a role alongside him in 1941's *Hold Back the Dawn*. After she scored a small role alongside Errol Flynn's title character in the James Corbett boxing biopic *Gentleman Jim* the next year, *Casablanca* and Yvonne's role as the lady cast aside by Rick Blaine came calling.

Sadly, Lebeau and Dalio divorced before *Casablanca*'s release. Dalio followed Humphrey Bogart through *To Have and Have Not* and *Sabrina* over the following decade. Lebeau made it all the way to within a month of her ninety-third birthday before she died in 2016, outliving all her *Casablanca* castmates.

Finally, right before the clock flipped to the a.m., long after someone of her age should have been snoozing, the ship's final passenger stepped off the *Quanza*. "I remember that my first impulse was to kiss the ground, but I didn't do it," Malvina Parnes said. "I'm not sure why I didn't kiss the ground, but when I think about it, I still get goosebumps. I still feel that feeling today."

Some got off the ship early enough to board a train up to New York that very evening. Others commandeered a bus. But for some, the local community didn't mind coming through one more time. Chuck Kaufman and his wife, Doris, were celebrating their anniversary that night, but this was something of an extenuating circumstance. Doris was one of several ladies who drove some passengers back to her home for the best sleep they'd had in months, maybe longer. Not surprisingly, so was Margolius. "At midnight," she recalled, "we all drove our cars to the ship and filled them to overflowing with people. Some were put up at the Fairfax Hotel. We took the rest home."

Others stayed with her neighbor Herbert Gerst, a successful laundromat owner whose own grandfather had stowed away from Germany to America in the midst of the Civil War. "My family took in a European family that spoke no English," explains Ed Lazaron, Herbert's grandson. "They were Orthodox Jews who ate kosher. The only thing they could eat was hard-boiled eggs that were boiled in a pan and peeled and not contaminated by milk or meat." The Gerst children sat down and painted and colored portraits of the refugees, gifting them as goodbye presents the next day. "Hitler said he was going to wipe out the Jewish race, and he did kill a lot of us," Gerst said. "I couldn't sit around making money and watch my people being destroyed."

A mother and daughter slept over at the Rosenberg household. "They had very few possessions," Rosenberg said. "They had small suitcases with a few clothes in it, and that was it. What did [the mother] want most of all? A cup of coffee. Real coffee, 'cause they had nothing but this ersatz stuff that was made of sawdust. They just poured down the dock, the gangway, and they kissed the ground. The smiles on their faces…were worth every bit of effort we put in."

> *It's essential that it's remembered that a community, a Southern Jewish community and members of it, both the Jews and non-Jews of that community, met the ship and welcomed them in, and the town welcomed them in that night.*
>
> —*Victoria Redel, author*

The next day, most of the newest Americans left. Jacob's brother Alan drove some of them, including the Rand family, to Washington. Others jumped on a bus to go there and, soon after, to New York. After spending days hoping the passengers would get to arrive, Margolius and others were thrilled to see them depart. "I can see their happy, smiling faces, waving American flags as they waved goodbye and the bus pulled away," she said. "We all just wept."

For Margolius, whose birthday was September 21, it was the most memorable of early birthday presents. She died in February 2002, seven months before her one hundredth birthday. She's buried in Norfolk's Forest Lawn Cemetery, just about five miles from the site of the *Quanza* matter.

Eleanor Roosevelt wished she could have been on the dock herself. Media coverage of the matter, which had grown steadily leading up to the passengers' release, would have turned into a Vesuvius-level eruption had the First Lady made an appearance. She didn't; she was still up in Hyde Park writing her daily newspaper column, aptly titled "My Day."

Just a few days later, however, she was in Chicago helping her son launch his burgeoning film career. After spending a few years working as an unofficial page and secretary for his father, James Roosevelt, who helped his father repeal Prohibition just a few months into his first term, had gone to Hollywood to work for legendary film producer Samuel Goldwyn. In 1940, he'd help distribute the British film *Pastor Hall*—ironically, a biopic about German clergyman Martin Niemoller, who was imprisoned for denouncing the Nazis. Niemoller is the author of the legendary "First They Came" poem that is inscribed on the United States Holocaust Memorial. Still interned when *Pastor Hall* was released, he was held at Dachau and Sachsenhausen before liberation. When the film made its way to America, many battled to censor it. But it was released, with an opening of Eleanor denouncing the Nazis. Once they got to New York, several passengers put together a card and flowers for her. "With everlasting gratitude for your human gesture," it read, "from the refugees of the SS *Quanza*." Eleanor left the gift outside her husband's bedroom.

> *My husband was thoroughly exhausted when it was all over, both mentally and physically, but we kept up our spirits, and in the end, the people were finally able to get off the ship. I just hope they can find comfort in our country after leaving everything behind.*
>
> —*Sallie Morewitz*

CHAPTER 16

LAST LEGAL ISSUES

Still, this might not be a permanent solution. The release order was worded in such a way, as is common in the legal world, that stated that things could start again at any time. Therefore, without actually saying so, this action could be considered only temporary. Any day, the newcomers could be called back, hauled into court, put on another ship (maybe the *Quanza*, which would be returning overseas soon) and even deported. They weren't officially in the clear.

Jacob and Sallie Morewitz didn't bother to hide their grins. Let local law enforcement go ahead and try that. They'd just been there and scored a victory—well, as much as one could in this situation—and would gleefully come back for round two. They'd convinced enough judges and lawyers that this was worth fighting for. Finding a group of Hampton Roads legal eagles willing to battle their own city-mates would be all but impossible.

Of course, if that did happen, there would be another contract breach charge coming. This time, they might ask for millions. Even the biggest shipbuilding companies would eventually decide that these little people weren't worth the trouble.

Still, quite a few were very nervous, certainly understandable after everything they'd been through.

"All were admitted," said Cecilia Razovsky, "with the understanding that they would leave the U.S. as promptly as they possibly could." Many did just that, at least for the time being. Some darted to Canada. Others went to South America. Even many of those who remained in America intentionally stayed in the background. Many changed their names. Some stayed home from synagogue services and did not openly celebrate Hanukkah, Passover, Yom Kippur or any other Jewish holidays.

Ironically enough, after its passengers, who had been held against their will, were off and away, the *Quanza* itself was now being held as an impromptu prisoner, unable to leave until its own bond was posted. But agents dished out $5,000 on September 16, and the ship shipped out the next day, on its way back to Lisbon. Hundreds had boarded for the initial voyage, dozens had been dropped off at a time and the passengers now numbered in the single digits. Along with a few *Quanza* passengers who'd unexpectedly decided to stay onboard and return home, José Asseca had come over from Lisbon to represent the *Quanza*'s overseeing company, Pinto Basto, in the legal battles, and now he was hitching a ride home.

As is typical for court action, Morewitz's libel suit went around and around the courts for years: appeals, authority issues, everything else that keeps verdicts from being finalized. Nearly three years later, when the *Quanza* folk had moved on and Jacob and Sallie had continued with one case after another, the final word came down. The Rands, who were by now operating a costume jewelry business in New York, had won the case, and they learned of their reward.

Zero. Not a dime. After all the filing, all the issuing, the testimonies, everything else, Judge Way finally ruled in January 1943 that the Rands, and the Morewitzes, simply weren't entitled to any further compensation. Had the suit not been filed, Judge Way (who, sadly, passed away the following October) wrote in the final argument,

> *that vessel would very probably have left that jurisdiction with the* [passengers] *on board. Where the vessel would have proceeded thereafter, no one can say....* [Passengers'] *conduct and all the evidence heard point to the fact that they had finally obtained the relief they really sought, namely, the privilege of going ashore and remaining in the United States and not having to go back to Europe, from which continent they were refugees fleeing to save their lives.*

Maybe just for his own personal pleasure, Jacob even appealed the decision. It didn't work. That was okay. The Rands' lives would be more than enough. Neither they nor any other passengers were ever asked, let alone required, to leave their new home. Over the next few years, many passengers made new lives for themselves in New York. Some waited until the war was over and then went back to Europe. For many, a sigh of final relief could finally be taken.

CHAPTER 17

JEWISH MILITARY HISTORY

Jews had long played a major role in the American military. In the Civil War, thousands fought and hundreds died from both the gray and the blue, several in all-Jewish companies. Underestimating the Jewish assistance his side enjoyed, Union General Ulysses S. Grant ordered that Jews be banned from Kentucky, Tennessee and Mississippi, but he was quickly overruled. President Lincoln helped appoint Philadelphia's Rodeph Shalom as the U.S. Army's first Jewish chaplain.

Edward Saloman, Frederick Knefler, Leopold Blumberg and Frederick Saloman were elevated to the rank of brigadier general by the Union. Judah Benjamin served as the Confederacy's attorney general, secretary of war and secretary of state during the war, later making it to Congress.

Thousands more would take part in the First World War, and the tale of William Shemin became one of the more notable ones from history. On the battlefields of France, the New Jersey teenager individually rescued several of his wounded colleagues and then, literally the next day, took command of his platoon when his superiors were killed. He'd win the Purple Heart and then the Distinguished Silver Cross. In 2015, three decades after his death, Shemin was awarded the Medal of Honor. Four years earlier, President Obama had signed the National Defense Authorization Act. Included in it was the William Shemin Jewish World War I Veterans Act, which allows the Pentagon to review the cases of Jews who may have been denied honors such as Shemin's for anti-Semitic reasons. Sadly, like Shemin, many Medal of Honor recipients had long since passed, some during battle themselves.

The Philippine Sea island of Saipan was launched into the world's public eye in the summer of 1944, when over twenty-five thousand were killed in the Battle of Saipan. That action and the D-Day attacks that occurred at the same time in France are seen as two of the last major points that turned the war all the way in the Allies' favor.

Ben Saloman was drafted in 1940 but was lucky enough to avoid active combat for the next few years. He'd been a practicing dentist before and during World War II; in the midst of combat, there wasn't much need for cavity filling.

The Saipan battle had been going for weeks now, and many knew, or hoped, that Japan's losses would get high enough for it to quit. But many from the Land of the Rising Sun would rather die in battle than raise any flags, and Saloman and his colleagues were about to see this firsthand. On the morning of July 7, Axis forces barreled forward. The front lines couldn't hold them back, and the Japanese soon made it to the aid station where Saloman and others were providing medical supplies to the wounded.

A soldier rushed into the tent. Saloman grabbed a rifle, blasted the man to the afterlife and ordered everyone else to run, carrying whatever or whoever they could. Now equipped with a machine gun, Saloman stood and fired at anything that moved. Moments later, he was all alone against hundreds, and he would stay that way. Only two days later, the conflict was over. Soon after that, troops finally got back to the site. They found Saloman's bullet- and bayonet-riddled body slumped over his gun. They also found nearly one hundred Axis reps he'd taken down before he died.

Soon after, Saloman was recommended to receive the Medal of Honor. The request was denied; the military cited the fact that medical officers could not receive medals. A second request was turned down in 1951; the excuse this time was that the time limit for such applications had passed. In 1969, Defense Secretary Melvin Laird, too busy dealing with the Vietnam War, again did not approve Saloman's honor. Finally, in 1998, another recommendation came through, and President Bush deemed Saloman worthy of the medal.

In the first days of 1945, Isadore Jachman and his company were pinned down in Belgium, their comrades dead all around them. It was less than a month after Jachman's twenty-second birthday, and he knew he wasn't getting out alive. Dodging a hail of bullets, Jachman charged over to a fallen friend and snatched the man's bazooka. Tanks and guns were firing on him, and some were hitting. But a man in that sort of position doesn't feel much at all. Blasting at the tanks, Jachman destroyed one. He disabled the other.

Then he fell for the last time. Today, a statue of him stands at that very site, and a Maryland armory is named after him.

In the summer of 1943, Raymond Zussman was part of the invasions of both North Africa and Italy. An injury gave him the option of spending the rest of the war in an office, but he refused. He belonged on the battlefield. In September 1944, four years after the *Quanza* matter, he commanded a tank through the streets, enemies shooting at and all around him. Zussman made it through that battle, but in the tragedy of irony, he was killed by a German bomb less than two weeks later. U.S. Army soldiers have trained in urban warfare at Fort Knox's Zussman Village since 1997, and several parks and playgrounds across Zussman's Michigan homeland bear his name.

Elsewhere during World War II, several prominent Jewish scientists, such as J. Robert Oppenheimer, Leo Szilard and a particularly notable fellow named Albert Einstein, were involved in the Manhattan Project, which resulted in the creation of the atomic bombs used in the war. Many later expressed regret for this work.

Overall, it's estimated that over 1 million Jews from around the world served during the Second World War. America, whose Jewish soldiers numbered between 500,000 and 550,000 during the war, made the largest individual contribution of Jewish soldiers as a country. About 52,000 American Jews received awards for their service.

CHAPTER 18

TRUMAN

By April 1945, the Axis powers were on their last war legs. The Soviet military had helped knock back the German blitzkrieg and decimated the country while the Nazis retreated. The United States, the Soviet Union and the rest of the Allies were moving in from every direction. The Soviets had liberated Auschwitz, and America had done so to Dachau, Buchenwald and other camps. Germany's war friends were deserting, Italy had already surrendered and there was nowhere to go but a loss.

Since the September before, America had already been coining the term *V-E Day* (Victory in Europe Day) as a way to commemorate the victory that Old Glory just knew was coming. But fate had one more dark obstacle to throw in America's way: on April 12, 1945, Franklin D. Roosevelt, the only president many Americans saw fit to elect four times, who'd turned the country around through the Great Depression and a war that looked unwinnable for much of the early 1940s, suddenly passed away.

With victory within its grasp, America now had to turn to someone whom few knew at all. Harry Truman had become vice president only at Roosevelt's fourth inauguration the previous January (John Nance Garner and Henry Wallace had been Roosevelt's vice presidents during his first three terms). Now a fellow who had openly stated he didn't want the Oval Office had a country to run and a World War to win. Fortunately, less than a month into his term, Truman got an early benefit from Roosevelt's and the military's hard work: Germany gave up in early May, and V-E Day came around. (Not until the following August did Truman deliver the war-ending atomic bombings of Japan, an act that will never stop being debated.)

As we all know, Hitler had already showed his own true colors of courage (or complete lack thereof), taking his own life before his country even quit, and his right-hand men Joseph Goebbels and Heinrich Himmler, two of the main forces behind the Holocaust, had followed suit in May. Not long after, as the true obscenities of the Final Solution continued to come to public light, Truman ensured that others who'd been behind the genocide would pay, helping to arrange the Nuremberg Trials, which would send twelve Nazis to their deaths and three more to lifetime imprisonment.

Truman, who would later usher America through the start of the Korean War and the Cold War, along with taking some of his country's first steps toward civil rights equality, long put a higher priority on carrying out hard decisions than on his public image—a rarity in American politics—which is part of the reason he set a sad record for the lowest approval ratings when leaving office in 1953. Fortunately, history has elevated him back up toward the top; a 2022 poll had him ranked in the top ten of all time.

On Truman's Oval Office desk stood a statement that many (again, at least in politics) pontificate but fewer actually act on: "The buck stops here." A president, Truman believed and usually showed, needs to have the guts to not only make certain decisions but also take responsibility for them when they don't work out. But this is about something else he once said and often practiced, much more than most politicians: "It's amazing what you can accomplish," Truman stated, "if you do not care who gets the credit."

This declaration would end up personifying the Morewitzes and their accomplishment. Since the *Quanza* pulled in to Norfolk, newspapers across the nation had been trying to outdo each other in finding out details about the ship, the passengers, the people on it, those trying to save them, their favorite radio programs and so on and so on. But when the Morewitzes and others won and the passengers made it to freedom, the climax, the major Earth-changing moment that so many expected to write about and so many more hoped to read about, didn't happen. The story had made it into every paper in Virginia, as far north as New York and Maine, down to Florida, over to California and even Canada and, of course, to Washington, D.C. But when the near-empty ship left port and headed to a different continent just a few days later, the coverage went with it. Good reporters can always find something to write about, and as a new World War raged closer to America, they had had enough of the *Quanza* story. Even the aftereffects of the *Quanza* matter, which are discussed later in this book, weren't brought up until much later, and even then, the resolution was barely minimal.

And the Morewitzes were just fine with that. Some lawyers don't mind seeing their names in print time and again (and on television, although that medium hadn't really taken off yet), but Jacob and Sallie did their promoting on behalf of their clientele, not themselves. "My grandparents were busy litigators," recalls Stephen Morewitz, "not like today, when lawyers have public relations emphasis. My grandfather always said, 'Just make sure the newspapers spell your name correctly.'" To be fair, this may have been a problem for journalists, especially outside Hampton Roads. "Morewitz" isn't quite on the level of "Smith" or "Jones" when it comes to wordsmanship. "He wasn't interested in being honored by the press," Morewitz continued. "Self-promotion was never a thing with my family. His name was in the papers sometimes, but he was not a media hound."

It's doubtful that by the end of September 1940, the pair were even recalling much about the *Quanza* affair. They certainly had more than enough to do, and they didn't waste time getting back into the legal game. There were other briefs to write, arguments to make, people to represent and cases to, usually, win. Not until the next year would they be finished with the *Edit H.* case, which had nearly caused them to have to turn down the *Quanza* matter. Three days after the Pearl Harbor attacks, Sallie attempted to calm the local Jewish community with a sermon at her synagogue in Newport News.

Once again, so long before their country entered World War II, the Morewitzes, like everyone else in America and much of the world, had little idea of what would have awaited the *Quanza* passengers had their case not been won. A few years later, when the depths of Nazi evil and the amount of time it had actually been going on came all the way into the public eye, Sallie and Jacob probably felt a serious sense of shock, sadness and, ultimately, pride about what they'd achieved, as did the rest of those who helped out the *Quanza* group.

In February 1942, the Morewitzes filed a new libel suit against owners of the Japanese steamship *Aspasia Nomikos* when it landed in Hampton Roads, on behalf of seven men who claimed they were underpaid and overworked in unsafe conditions aboard the ship. Ironically, their suit for $7,000 caused a delay for a ship carrying over $300,000 worth of sugar.

Four years later, the Greek ship *88 Olympos* landed at Sewell's Point to fill up on coal, just as the *Quanza* had. And just like before, Jacob was ready. Thirteen members of the crew had walked off the ship after working in conditions that Jacob himself deemed "shocking," and he'd go on to win a libel suit on their behalf. In March 1962, he argued successfully before the Supreme Court on behalf of Clifford Vaughan, a seaman who'd been denied pay by his ship's owner after being discharged for having tuberculosis.

Still, very quickly, the *Quanza* matter faded away. Maybe people felt that rescuing just a few dozen people wasn't a big enough deal; had it been hundreds, maybe history would appreciate it more. The Morewitzes' desire to avoid credit probably played a role, especially since such a sentiment was clearly shared by many of their legal colleagues who'd been involved in the *Quanza* issue. Furthermore, the fact that many of the passengers chose to scatter quickly and not stay in touch made a coherent story difficult to tell.

For years, the *Quanza* tale might have gotten nothing more than a sentence in a few history texts and textbooks here and there. Strangely, ship enemy Breckinridge Long's diaries, which were published in 1966, told more of the story than most pieces before or since, albeit an obviously biased version.

In 1990, a full half-century after the ship landed and left, Jacob and Sallie's grandson Stephen Morewitz started receiving some messages and documents. His uncle David had been researching David's parents' work for the past few years, and he hoped Stephen, himself the proud owner of a PhD from the University of Chicago, might help him tell the story. Stephen knew just where to go and who to ask. He happened to live right near Susan Lieberman. "She said, 'I'm a playwright,'" Stephen says. "I said, 'I have a play for you.'" He read David's materials on the matter. He looked over Long's writings.

Many theatrical productions had told the story of the Holocaust; one of the watershed examples, *The Diary of Anne Frank*, reached Broadway in 1955 and won a Tony for Best Play the next year. However, Stephen says, "This was the first play about the American response to refugees from Hitler's Europe being let into America. Once I discovered Breckenridge Long's history and his involvement, I realized this was a big story that had been submerged, for the most part." In 1991, he and Lieberman opened their play *Steamship Quanza* at the Chicago Dramatists Workshop. In the play, Eleanor Roosevelt makes an appearance, as do (of course) the Morewitzes, the Rands and even attempted "swimaway" Wolff, albeit under different names. Critics loved it, audiences loved it and it ran for over thirty years.

Sadly, by this point, the Morewitzes weren't around to see their story told. Sallie died in August 1974, and Jacob followed nine years later. In 1992, Stephen and the rest of the family accepted a posthumous honor from the Jewish Community Federation of Richmond and the Virginia Historical Society. They also received a similar honor from a Connecticut organization.

It's tough to go too far into a story when most of its details have been forgotten, misplaced or hidden. Stephen wouldn't be the only one to encounter this problem. "When my book came out, I was invited to speak at Long Island University," remembered Victoria Redel, who taught at Columbia University and eventually moved to Sarah Lawrence College. "There was an exhibition about ships that had been lost, turned back or torpedoed. Until I was invited to speak, the curators hadn't heard about the plight of the *Quanza*. The *St. Louis* was more well known."

Maybe it was fate. It might have been her secret muse, so great at stunning with sudden bursts of realization, inspiration and creativity. Walking down the street in New York City one day, Redel heard something. "Dear Eleanor Roosevelt," her mind suddenly whispered, "do you like stories?" Sometimes, such a whisper is all an author needs. Starting off with the very words she'd silently heard, her book began as a set of letters to the First Lady from Itzak Rejdel. Stranded at the Norfolk docks with the rest of the *Quanza* group, Rejdel had little to do but obsessively write his letters.

"I first started thinking about it probably in 2003," Redel remembers of her next literary adventure. "I'm a novelist, so the notion of a journey is a pretty natural trajectory, and a journey that has obstruction along the way is novelistic. I decided not to think about writing a family history or a memoir but to have it be a fiction, with freedom to create complicated characters and their situation."

As Redel told his story for the first few chapters, that's how it stayed. The manuscript was already using biographical elements—the character of Itzak was named for her own father, who'd been on the ship with his own parents. "My father was a great source of research for the book," Redel says. "I thought the book was going to be called *Dear Eleanor Roosevelt* and that it was just going to consist of letters from Itzak to Eleanor. Then, as novels do, it shifted and began to have a contemporary component, where I began to think about: *Who would be the daughter of this man? What would she know?* I decided to have her be the detective of her father's life."

The book began to switch back and forth between Itzak's letters (he had some secrets of his own) and the tale of modern-day Manhattan translator Sara, who was balancing her plan to adopt a child with the secrets she'd started to uncover about her own father's past and her understanding of New York as a home for so many refugees. As the story went on, the connection between the two tales became, slowly and surely, apparent. Finally, in 2007, *The Border of Truth* was published.

While Redel and Stephen Morewitz incorporated their own personal creativity into their written works, Laura Seltzer-Duny chose to go the visually factual route. About a year after PBS viewers saw her (along with narrator Sam Waterston, known for his work on *Law & Order*) tell the sad tale of the endangered Chesapeake Bay in *The Last Boat Out*, David and Stephen approached their cousin with a new proposal. "David and Stephen Morewitz came to me and said, 'Hey, we hear you make documentaries,'" said Seltzer-Duny, who grew up near the Morewitzes' Newport News offices. "This is definitely a documentary in broad context that affected a lot of the decisions to do with refugees after the ship came in and they closed the doors."

"Nobody wants us." After being kicked out of their own homeland and being denied entrance to two countries, this was the mantra that so many *Quanza* passengers sadly recited to themselves and each other for months. It became the title of Seltzer-Duny's film, which allowed what few passengers remained as of the early 2010s to tell the story themselves.

For about two years, Seltzer-Duny contacted survivors, those who helped them and everyone else she could reach who was there for those few precious days and weeks. Videos, photos, illustrations and, of course, interviews told the story in a way that hadn't been done before. The film won festival awards, including at several Jewish-specific festivals, in 2019 and 2020 and was nominated for an Emmy.

"The more I researched and spoke to the few remaining direct witnesses to the *Quanza* incident, the more I was eager to give voice to their story," Seltzer-Duny said. "The more I learned, the more I just fell in love with the story of what communities can do, what individuals can do, what church groups can do. These lawyers helped save over eighty lives. What an important, little-known story about unsung heroes during World War II."

But not everyone felt that way. Like many of those who have survived war, no matter in what capacity, the passengers, whom some would consider all but prisoners themselves, weren't eager to share their stories. Not that they were ashamed, but they were concerned about appearing a little too proud. "A lot of people, like Irving Redel, said, 'Why are you making this film? We survived, and all those people did not. That's the tragedy you should focus on. Don't focus on us. We survived,'" Seltzer-Duny remembered. "Their mindset was survivor's guilt. A lot of Holocaust survivors feel that way. 'Don't worry about my story. Worry about my brothers and sisters who never made it out.'"

CHAPTER 19

AN UNHAPPY ENDING

We survived, and that is fine. Six million did not survive, and that is the catastrophe.
—Quanza *passenger Irving Redel*

If only the story had ended there, with the *Quanza* passengers strolling off and into a land and life of prosperity, living happily ever after in the utopian melting pot America has always subtly portrayed itself to be.

Actually, in a just world, that wouldn't have been all. Instead, word and joy would have spread across America and maybe even made their way back to Europe: America had become the land to welcome those who simply wanted their freedom and were brave enough to ask for it. Those called for by Lady Liberty herself would have finally gotten a new chance to take the deepest breath and feel freedom rush into their lungs and throughout their bodies.

And so would many more, right? Hundreds, thousands, however large the welcome numbers could reach would rise up and roll away from their tormentors back in Europe, off to a welcome new home, somewhere in North America or elsewhere, safe from the unspeakable evil that was starting to sweep over Germany. The *Quanza* story and those who helped write it could have been the first chapter in a piece showing the love and strength of humanity. That would be a happy ending. It would be a true American story.

But this is real life, and as the world would find out so many times throughout the 1940s, truth is sadder and scarier than what we want, what we dream of. Despite the courageous tale that has, hopefully, inspired us over the previous pages and chapters, this story doesn't have the conclusion it deserves.

"Why me?" There's a stereotype, perhaps as far as a stigma, that gets attached to that question. Sometimes when we hear others ask it or even ask it to ourselves—usually silently—it's because things are going too far wrong for us to even comprehend, or so we think. But it can also go the other way. Sometimes we ask it in sadness, draped in sorrow even when the good happens. It's not that we don't appreciate our positive fortune. It's that sometimes we feel like we were too lucky. We made it, we thrived, but others didn't and never would. Thousands, maybe millions, have been asking that question since the Holocaust began. Those who lived to ask it were lucky. They knew it. But so many others should have been just as fortunate, and no one could ever know why.

Even the survivors of the most inhumane acts in world history walked away with a certain type of shame. Their families, their friends, even those they never knew, who could and would have done amazing things, were gone forever. Decades later, those who made it out and away felt so small in comparison to the innocents who deserved to do so, maybe even more than they themselves did.

> *The* Quanza *case seems to nullify the attempt of Congress to prevent the entry of those Europeans trying to come to the United States. Under the interpretation of the Department of Justice in this case, we could admit the total populations of Czechoslovakia, France, Belgium, Holland, Denmark, and Norway.*
>
> *—Colgate Darden, Virginia congressman (1933–37, 1939–41) and governor (1942–46)*

The SS *Quanza* matter could have kicked off a wonderful movement that just might have saved so many others from the human plague rolling across their homeland. Instead, it became a different kind of beginning, a beginning of the end—and the end started soon and lasted for far too long.

Still seething over losing the battle to send the *Quanza* folk back, Breckinridge Long decided to go all out to win the war against immigration. He thought that only a few would get into Norfolk, mainly children and pregnant women. When Malin told him that all passengers were being allowed to land, Long nearly went through the ceiling of the State, War, and Navy Building. Not only was his own government opening the door to potential spies, now and in the future, but someone was also undercutting his authority. Long said,

> *As soon as it became known that they were to arrive at Norfolk, I was flooded with pressure groups and telegrams and personal visits to permit the landing of persons off of the boat. I consistently declined to deviate from the procedure which we had adopted and said that the fact that the people were on the boat and were nearing the American shores did not constitute an emergency of any kind.*

Now it was personal. And many people suffered and died because it became so personal. With a little help from his cautious friends, Long pushed through some legislation that doomed an unknown number of innocents to become prisoners in their own land. He claimed:

> *We have been very generous in offering hospitality in the United States to persons who have been in imminent danger there, who have been leaders of public thought. I have felt that the procedure of extending visas to persons in the categories indicated* [rabbis and labor leaders] *was a perfectly legitimate practice, provided the bars were not thrown down to the extent that the categories were expanded and a lot of persons admitted to the United States in contravention of the law.…A departure from this practice would be in effect to render the immigration laws negatory.*
>
> *I remonstrated violently* [and] *said that I thought that* [the act] *was a violation of the law, not in accord with my understanding with them, not a proper interpretation of my agreement, that I would not be party to it, that I would not give my consent, that I would have no responsibility for it, and that if they did that, I would have to take the matter up some other way.*

He did. A mere four days after refugees disembarked in Norfolk, Long got approval from both Secretary of State Cordell Hull and Roosevelt himself to terminate the emergency visa program, removing authority from the President's Committee on Political Refugees to issue emergency visas. This slammed shut the door on the rabbis, intellectuals and labor leaders who might have gotten these visas. As persecution of Jews and other Nazi enemies intensified in Europe, Long's actions made it even more difficult for refugees to escape to America.

"The list of rabbis has been closed and the list of labor leaders has been closed," he said on September 18, 1940, "and now it remains for the

President's Committee to be curbed in its activities so that the laws again can operate in their normal course. It is intended not, repeat not, to have any further incidents occur at an American port similar to the *Quanza*."

James McDonald, who had fought so hard for German refugees in the 1930s, tried to convince Roosevelt to change his mind but was unsuccessful. In 1949, President Truman appointed McDonald the first American ambassador to Israel, and his personal papers hold a place today in the United States Holocaust Memorial Museum.

In a weird way, the *Quanza* folk had found themselves in the wrong place at the wrong time, as their arrival and release gave the political higher-ups a jumping-off point to do everything but build a brick wall up and down the border. Still, any guilt they, or anyone else, may have felt about it was undeserved. A man as determined as Long was willing to cut any corner, stab any back, take advantage of anyone already in an unthinkably hard situation to get what he wants. It was nothing these few dozen individuals who'd fought for the *Quanza* folk, the Morewitzes or anyone else did on a personal level: Long just needed an excuse to start working his black magic. If the *Quanza* had been turned away, another ship would have eventually gotten through, and Long would have used it as his personal reason to put his own interests above those of so many others. The *Quanza* crew just happened to show up and get many people to say yes. It was no one's fault that other people, more powerful people, said no for a long time afterward.

While people like the Morewitzes and others who stepped up to save the *Quanza* group were on the best of missions, Long was on the worst. "Each one of these men hates me," Long said of his opponents (and so many others for generations to come). "I am to them the embodiment of a nemesis. They each and all believe every person, everywhere, has a right to come to the United States. I believe nobody, anywhere, has a right to enter the United States unless the United States desires."

By 1942, overseas passenger transportation had been all but suspended in North America. The *Quanza* was one of the few exceptions, but its owners chose compensation over compassion. As one of the only games in town, the company felt free to charge passengers whatever it wanted and drove ticket fees up until they were the highest in world history. For the same trip that the refugees had taken in 1940, the cheapest prices on the *Quanza* became as much as $1,300. Today, that's over $25,000—again, per ticket, for the lowest conditions. The top-class group would be charged around $2,500 per ticket, which goes all the way up past $48,000 in today's dollars.

America started tightening its quotas on immigration—and then not even coming close to fulfilling them. Mere months before Pearl Harbor reached out and yanked the United States into the war, American consulates in Nazi-occupied territories (yes, even by then, we still weren't entirely against them) were preventing many from issuing visas. Soon after, the U.S. State Department arranged for a special committee in Washington, D.C., to approve all visas, which made things even harder for those trying to escape. Many, far too many, simply ran out of time. Even as America spent its bloodiest years in the war from 1942 to 1945, less than 10 percent of the German refugees who applied to come to Old Glory made it. And Long was a major reason why. "If Long lost the *Quanza* battle," admitted Holocaust historians Allan Lichman and Richard Breitman, "he quietly won the war on refugees."

It wouldn't be until after the war that the remainder of the world, including much of Germany, would learn the horrifying true extent of the Holocaust. Thousands of Jews who were turned away from America became its victims. Not until January 1944 did Roosevelt establish the War Refugee Board (Cordell Hull was a member), stressing that it was to "take action for the immediate rescue from the Nazis of as many as possible of the persecuted minorities of Europe—racial, religious, or political—all civilian victims of enemy savagery." Among other actions, the board sent millions of dollars in relief (a number not adjusted for inflation) to concentration camp prisoners and those hiding from and battling the Holocaust (weaponry was provided as well) and convinced many neutral countries to accept Jewish refugees. Long, who lost most of his authority when the board was established, labeled it "a good move for political reasons." That November, he resigned and retired.

Yes, the board's actions looked good on paper, especially in the pages of history books. Yes, it sounds like something to be proud of. But it was far too little and far too late. Not for a full year after the board's creation, after an immeasurable number of deaths there and elsewhere, would Auschwitz, the most infamous concentration camp in history, be liberated, and the Soviet Union did the hard work there. In April and May 1945, American troops liberated several other camps, including Dachau.

Frances Perkins left behind a much brighter legacy than Long. She held the secretary of labor position for twelve years, longer than anyone else before or since, and left by choice, electing to resign after Roosevelt's death (she'd been a major contributor to his New Deal and was a driving force behind establishing Social Security and unemployment insurance). She served on the United States Civil Service Commission and on the faculty of Cornell

University. In 1980, fifteen years after her death, the New Labor Building, the Labor Department headquarters just up the road from the White House, was renamed the Frances Perkins Building.

Cordell Hull also brightened his own legacy, his eleven-year term as secretary of state the longest in history. After helping to create the United Nations, he won the Nobel Prize in 1945.

In 1962, at her Manhattan home during her final days, Eleanor Roosevelt, who may have become America's first female president if she'd chosen to run, called her failure to help more refugees "her deepest regret at the end of her life," said her son Jimmy.

The *Quanza* would continue its shipping ways, carrying supplies up and down its regular route and occasionally bringing some human cargo to America before being scrapped in Spain in 1966. A film and a small exhibit on the *Quanza* matter would eventually show up in the United States Holocaust Museum in Washington, D.C.

> *More could have been saved, hundreds of thousands more, but died. It was a missed opportunity. Over a million could have made it.*
>
> —*Harry Morewitz, son of Sallie and Jacob*

As the war went on, and even after it ended, many involved in the *Quanza* matter couldn't help but blame themselves, feeling that they were luckier than they deserved. In this way, they were like many veterans, who went overseas to fight the war itself and had to come home without their friends—and some powerful depression came with them. For many, it never went away, just as it still doesn't for today's military community. It might not seem fair, but it's a dark reality of human nature.

"He had tremendous survivor's guilt his whole life," Kathleen Rand recalls of her dad, Wolff, who lived all the way to ninety-seven. "I tried to get stories out of him, but he didn't want to talk about any of it. He was a very quiet man."

Yes, there are far too many dark clouds blotting out the end of this story. But as we come to the end of our own tale, let's do what we can to focus on the smallest of silver linings. Rather than focus on what came later and what didn't happen, let's end by remembering what was done right, what people could control and did—and did so well.

"How should they be remembered?" wondered Chip Goldstein, himself a Newport News lawyer and longtime treasurer of the Rodef Sholom Temple, to which the Morewitzes belonged.

> *We heard about this occasionally when we were growing up, and I was surprised we didn't know more about it. We should know the story. It's more than just folklore; it's inspiration. It's two people that saved all those people. What opportunity do you have in this life to save a literal shipload of people? Jacob acted. He saw people in need, and he did what he thought he could do. He was willing to fall on his face and fall on his dagger, but he was willing to go to the mat for all those people, all those families. I would like to think that I would have had the strength and character to do what he did.*
>
> *Jacob Morewitz was like, "This is my job, and I'm not going to brag about what I did." Malin felt that way, too. No, guys, you were really standing up for the right thing in history.*
>
> —*Laura Seltzer-Duny*

A few dozen people were rescued from the *Quanza* and, therefore, the Holocaust. Those rescued chose not to stay in touch afterward, but judging by the numbers, we can assume, six decades later, that the list of descendants from that group has risen into the three figures, probably the high ones. Someday it'll get into the thousands, if it hasn't already, and the people involved in saving the *Quanza* passengers, along with their own descendants, will keep having more and more reasons to be proud. This many people are alive today because of the hard work and kindness of so many strangers.

Even with all the negativity—most of it undeserved—that we've discussed over the previous pages, with the tale of the *Quanza* comes a message of inspiration. It began back in Europe, when dozens of people, thrust up against indescribable evil, had the foresight and the wherewithal to fight back and escape. It continued on the trip, when the crew became an impromptu team, facing so much opposition and never giving up, no matter who or what stood against them. And it continued with the next makeshift squad that, with little personal gratification to be found, came together here in America to help them. People who showed courage. People who found some strength and compassion for many they'd never seen before or even heard of—and never would again after the matter ended. Those who stood up for them. Those who took them in and helped them move on. Those who just learned of their plight a few days before and roared into action, even if they didn't immediately know where to go, who to talk to or what to say. People who worked so hard, with little to no compensation or recognition (aside from books like this one and films like

Nobody Wants Us, which they obviously couldn't control) before or after, people who just did a hard job that was the right thing to do and then went on with their lives. These people, their own descendants and those who are alive today because of them can affirm their own success.

Credit and confirmation by others do not make us exceptional. It's what people do, and the lessons we can learn, the qualities we can recognize, take away and find within ourselves to use in our lives one day that make us better people. And in so many ways, the story of the *Quanza* shows us how.

BIBLIOGRAPHY

Barnidge, Mary Shen. "Steamship *Quanza*." *Chicago Reader*, June 20, 1991. https://chicagoreader.com/arts-culture/steamship-quanza.

Blakemore, Erin. "A Ship of Jewish Refugees Was Refused U.S. Landing in 1939. This Was Their Fate." History, June 4, 2019. https://www.history.com/news/wwii-jewish-refugee-ship-st-louis-1939.

Boston Daily Globe. "Clinton Man, Freed by Germans, Warns Against Fifth Column." August 20, 1940.

Breitman, Richard, and Allan J. Lichtman. *FDR and the Jews*. Harvard University Press, 2013.

Buckley, Cara. "Fleeing Hitler, and Finding a Reluctant Miss Liberty." *New York Times*, July 8, 2007.

Cohen Center for Holocaust and Genocide Studies at Keene State College. "MS *St. Louis* Crisis." https://www.keene.edu/academics/cchgs/resources/documents/st-louis/download.

College of William & Mary Law School. "Books Given to Library in Memory of Jacob L. and Sallie Rome Morewitz." *Marshall-Whyte Update* 2, no. 1 (Spring 1988): 4.

Crews, Edward R. "Sanctuary." *Richmond Law* 10, no. 2 (Summer 1997): 10–13.

Daily Press (Newport News, VA). "File Libel in Ship Case; 13 Crewman Paid." October 4, 1947.

———. "Habeas Corpus Writ Sworn Out to Get Sailors Off Ship." September 17, 1924.

———. "Hurricane of Legal Action Stops Sailing of Ship with 83 Refugees as Passengers." September 12, 1940.

———. "Local Case Argued in Supreme Court." November 7, 1929.

———. "Mrs. Jacob Morewitz Succumbs at Age 77." August 9, 1974.

———. "Notes Appeal in Old Libel Action." January 25, 1943.

———. "Post Bonds in Quanza Libels." September 17, 1940.

———. "Quanza Case Before Court." September 16, 1940.

———. "Quanza Sails for Lisbon." September 18, 1940.

———. "Roxen Libelled for Big Damages by Detained Men." September 18, 1924.

Daily Times. "War Refugees Held on Vessel." September 14, 1940.

Daniels, Lisa. "Group Honors Newport News Lawyer Posthumously." *Daily Press* (Newport News, VA), May 2, 1992.

Dearborn, Keri. *Eleanor Roosevelt: A Life in American History*. ABC-CLIO, 2022.

Evening Star. "Refugees Aboard Ship at Norfolk Start Suits for Release." September 12, 1940.

———. "U.S. Will Decide Whether to Let in Any of 89 on the Quanza." September 13, 1940.

Foreman, Adam, and Dayla Meyer. "American Nazism and Madison Square Garden." National WWII Museum, April 14, 2021. https://www.nationalww2museum.org/war/articles/american-nazism-and-madison-square-garden.

Freelance-Star (Fredericksburg, VA). "Many of Those on Ship at Norfolk May Get Permission." September 13, 1940.

Goldstein, Chip. Phone interview. August 6, 2024.

Goodman, Bonnie K. "Remembering the Jewish Refugees Aboard the Ill-Fated *St. Louis* 80 Years Later." *Times of Israel*, June 1, 2019. https://blogs.timesofisrael.com/remembering-the-jewish-refugees-aboard-the-ill-fated-st-louis-80-years-later.

Goodwin, Doris Kearns. *No Ordinary Time*. Simon & Schuster, 1994.

Hawthorne, Stephanie. "Harbored: Like Museum, Video Games Aren't Neutral." PhD dissertation, Old Dominion University, 2019.

Hodge, B. "Assistant Secretary of State Breckinridge Long and American Immigration Policy." PhD dissertation, Lamar University, 2012.

Holocaust Memorial Day Trust. "The SS St. Louis." 2024. https://www.hmd.org.uk/resource/ss-st-louis.

Jewish Virtual Library. "FDR Statement on Kristallnacht." https://www.jewishvirtuallibrary.org/fdr-statement-on-kristallnacht.

———. "U.S. Policy During the Holocaust: The Tragedy of the SS St. Louis." https://www.jewishvirtuallibrary.org/the-tragedy-of-s-s-st-louis.

———. "The War Refugee Board: Executive Order Creating the War Refugee Board." https://www.jewishvirtuallibrary.org/executive-order-creating-the-war-refugee-board-january-1944.

Johnson, Erskine. "In Hollywood." *Chico Enterprise*, March 6, 1944.

Kirschner, Sheldon. "Nobody Wants Us." Sheldon Kirshner Journal, September 25, 2020. https://sheldonkirshner.com/nobody-wants-us.

LaFranchi, Howard. "U.S. Immigration and Families: A Tale from the Holocaust Era." *Christian Science Monitor*, August 22, 2019.

Lanchin, Mike. "SS St Louis: The Ship of Jewish Refugees Nobody Wanted." BBC, May 13, 2014. https://www.bbc.com/news/magazine-27373131.

Ledger-Star. "Ship Leaves Aliens Here." August 31, 1940.

Long, Breckinridge. *The War Diary of Breckinridge Long: Selections from the Years 1939–1941*. University of Nebraska Press, 1966.

Lowrence, Dee. "Exquisite Extroverts." *Sacramento Union*, November 7, 1943.

Mazur, Eric Michael. "The SS *Quanza*, Jewish Refugees, and the Port of Hampton Roads, 1940." *Virginia Magazine of History and Biography* 130, no. 1 (2022): 38–78.

Medoff, Rafael. *America and the Holocaust*. Jewish Publication Society, 2022.

———. *The Jews Should Keep Quiet: Franklin D. Roosevelt, Rabbi Stephen S. Wise, and the Holocaust*. Jewish Publication Society, 2019.

Meier, Andrew. "'The God-Damnedest Thing': The Antisemitic Plot to Thwart U.S. Aid to Europe's Jews and the Man Who Exposed It." *Politico*, September 23, 2022.

Miami Daily News. "40 French Refugees May Land in U.S." September 14, 1940.

Montclair Times. "Ripley Anxious to Aid Britons." August 23, 1940.
Morewitz, Stephen. "The Saving of the SS Quanza." *William and Mary Magazine* (Summer 1991): 25–30.
Moskovits, Shlomo. "The United States Recognition of Israel in the Context of the Cold War, 1945–1948." PhD dissertation, Kent State University, 1976.
Paust, Matthew. "Jews Fleeing Nazis Made Freedom Flight." *Daily Press*, September 14, 1940.
Pizzo, Anthony. "Yvonne, or *Casablanca* in One Character and Three Scenes." Solute, August 21, 2014. https://www.the-solute.com.
Plunka, G.A. *Staging Holocaust Resistance.* Palgrave Studies in Theatre and Performance History. Palgrave Macmillan, 2012.
Prince, Cathryn. "Nearly Turned Back, a Ship of Holocaust Refugees Got Help from Eleanor Roosevelt." *Times of Israel*, August 15, 2019.
Richmond News Leader. "Darden Asks Why 86 Land." October 28, 1940.
———. "Not to Land." September 11, 1940.
Richmond Times-Dispatch. "Refugee Ship Due to Reach Norfolk Today." September 11, 1940.
———. "Refugees Take Legal Action to Stay Here." September 12, 1940.
———. "U.S. Officers Study Status of Refugees." September 13, 1940.
Roanoke Times. "Fast-Moving Attorneys Prevent Ship from Leaving Norfolk With Refugees." September 12, 1940.
Rochester Democrat and Chronicle. "U.S. Ambulance Drivers Home from Nazi Prison Camp." August 22, 1940.
Rodrigues, Janette. "Remembering." *Daily Press* (Newport News, VA), January 3, 1991.
Rudee, Eliana. "Eleanor Roosevelt's Efforts to Save Jewish Refugees from the Holocaust." *Jewish News Syndicate*, August 20, 2019. https://www.jns.org/eleanor-roosevelt-and-her-valiant-effort-to-save-jewish-refugees-from-the-holocaust.
Schaad, Tom. "Taken In: Jewish Refugees and Their Search for Asylum in Norfolk." WAVY, November 14, 2019. https://www.wavy.com.
Schleck, Dave. "Rough Sail to Freedom." *Daily Press* (Newport News, VA), February 14, 1998.
UIUC RBML Staff. "Collection Relating to the SS Quanza, 1995–2000." Rare Book & Manuscript Library, University of Illinois at Urbana-Champaign, 2017. https://archon.library.illinois.edu/rbml/?p=collections/findingaid&id=448&q=&rootcontentid=101932.
Valley Morning Star. "Noted Europeans Banned in Mexico Despite Their Visas." September 7, 1940.
Vegh, Steven. "Ship's Saga Is Part of Southern Jewish History." *Virginian-Pilot*, November 23, 2001.
Virginian-Pilot. "Most of Refugee Passengers on Quanza May Land Today." September 14, 1940.
———. "Refugee Ship Is Target of Many Suits." September 12, 1940.
———. "Sugar Laden Vessel Sails." February 10, 1942.
Washington Post. "U.S. to Check Ship Holding 4 Refugees: Habeas Corpus Plea Filed by Belgians to Gain Release." September 13, 1940.
———. "War Refugees, Turned Back, Sob as Ship Coals at Norfolk." September 12, 1940.

ABOUT THE AUTHOR

Jason Norman is an award-winning journalist and an English professor at both Old Dominion University and Norfolk State University in Norfolk, Virginia.